The Resurrection Stories

Zacchaeus Studies: New Testament

General Editor: Mary Ann Getty, RSM

The Resurrection Stories

by

Jerome H. Neyrey, S.J.

Michael Glazier
Wilmington, Delaware

About the Author

Jerome H. Neyrey, S.J., was educated at St. Louis University (BA, MA), Regis College, Toronto (MDiv and MTh), and Yale University (PhD). He is currently Associate Professor of New Testament at the Weston School of Theology, Cambridge, Massachusetts, and is on the editorial board of *Biblical Theology Bulletin* and the Catholic Biblical Quarterly. Among his publications is *Christ Is Community: The Christologies of the New Testament.*

First published in 1988 by Michael Glazier, Inc. 1935 West Fourth Street, Wilmington, Delaware, 19805. Copyright © 1988 by Michael Glazier, Inc. All rights reserved.

Library of Congress Catalog Card Number: 88-82446
International Standard Book Numbers:
    Zacchaeus Studies New Testament: 0-89453-662-1
    Resurrection Stories: 0-89453-664-8

Cover Design by Maureen Daney
Printed in the United States of America by Town House Press

TABLE OF CONTENTS

Editor's Note

Zacchaeus Studies provide concise, readable and relatively inexpensive scholarly studies on particular aspects of scripture and theology. The New Testament section of the series presents studies dealing with focal or debated questions; and the volumes focus on specific texts of particular themes of current interest in biblical interpretation. Specialists have their professional journals and other forums where they discuss matters of mutual concern, exchange ideas and further contemporary trends of research; and some of their work on contemporary biblical research is now made accessible for students and others in *Zacchaeus Studies*.

The authors in this series share their own scholarship in non-technical language, in the areas of their expertise and interest. These writers stand with the best in current biblical scholarship in the English-speaking world. Since most of them are teachers, they are accustomed to presenting difficult material in comprehensible form without compromising a high level of critical judgment and analysis.

The works of this series are ecumenical in content and purpose and cross credal boundaries. They are designed to augment formal and informal biblical study and discussion. Hopefully they will also serve as texts to enhance and supplement seminary, university and college classes. The series will also aid Bible study groups, adult education and parish religious education classes to develop intelligent, versatile and challenging programs for those they serve.

Mary Ann Getty RSM
New Testament Editor

Preface

This study of the Easter mystery of our Christian faith focuses on the stories in which the Risen Jesus manifests himself to his apostles and disciples. For reasons of space, other stories pertaining to Easter, such as the empty tomb, cannot be treated here. There are, of course, many perspectives from which a Christian reader might view these narratives of the appearances of the Risen Jesus. Traditionally, we have tended to emphasize historical questions: Did Jesus on that first Easter evening appear in Jerusalem (Luke and John) or in Galilee (Matthew)? Who was there and what really happened? Historical questions, while obviously important, are not the only, and maybe not the most pastoral line of inquiry for the believing reader. One might ask what meaning the appearances have, both for the original audiences of the gospel narratives and for us as well. What function did they serve? What aspect of Christology might be emphasized? What might the narratives tell us about the shape and structure of the early church? It is this latter set of questions that make up the perspective of this inquiry.

In contemporary biblical scholarship, this approach is labeled redaction criticism, for it focuses on the particular way each evangelist told the gospel story, with attention to the characteristic themes, motifs, vocabulary and social context of both the author and the church addressed. While not depreciating historical questions, at present we are not trying to recover the exact historical details of the Easter events. Of interest to us is the pastoral theology encoded in each narrative. Matthew's version of Jesus' appearance may not suit the needs of Luke's church, any more than Luke's version fits the situation which Paul addressed or to which John wrote. For, as we have come to learn about our Christian Scriptures, they are first and foremost the preaching or interpretation of Jesus by the evangelists for the life of the early communities gathered in his name. There are, moreover, four gospels, not one, and the distinctiveness of each has come to be seen as a rich treasure of faith, a treasure never more valuable than in a serious inquiry into the resurrection stories, which are themselves the foundations of our faith. This perspective, while perhaps new to some readers, has matured in our church and was formally endorsed in the Vatican II *Document on Revelation,* 19.

Specifically, this means that we will view the resurrection stories in terms of the special categories which biblical scholars employ regularly in their study of Scripture. We can learn much from asking about the literary shape of a narrative or its "form," for this can tell us the specific function a piece of literature had for its audience. The context of a story, its place in the narrative, is another important clue to its meaning. Each version of Jesus' Easter appearances is told from the particular viewpoint of each evangelist, which means we must learn to be sensitive to the particular themes, vocabulary etc. of each document, for the meaning of the story is conveyed in and through these details.

Finally, we must ask about the way Jesus is presented in the resurrection stories, what titles are given him, what powers, what role vis-à-vis his apostles and disciples, which is the focus of the category of "Christology" in the following chapters. This also means that we are as interested in the church which Jesus gathered around him and how the Easter stories tell us something about that church: to whom did Jesus appear? why appear to them? what charter might he have given the church at that time? One can never ask questions about Jesus without at the same time asking questions about the community which gathered in his name, for in a real sense Christ is community. This is the area of interest covered by the label "Ecclesiology" in this study. "Christology" and "Ecclesiology" are the two perspectives which help us to grasp how gospel stories are truly preachings about Jesus to specific churches, and how the gospels themselves are basically pastoral documents. Although these ways of reading a text may at first sound quite technical, they are the exciting perspectives which open the material to the inquiring mind and lead it to fresh and fruitful insights.

But what stories and what documents ought to be treated in a brief, but fundamental study of the topic? We have decided to concentrate on "stories" of Jesus' resurrection appearances, which means that we will not be able to talk about the various formulae used to interpret the risen Jesus. Rather, the focus is on the narrative stories of Jesus' appearances to his apostles and disciples. The document which deserves our initial attention is the oldest story of the Easter appearances, 1 Corinthians, which is not only one of the oldest documents in the New Testament, but contains still older popular formulae about important matters, such as material about the Eucharist (11:23ff) and the Resurrection (15:3-8). Next the gospel stories of Jesus' appearances come naturally to mind. Jesus' appearances in Mt 28, Lk 24 and John 20-21 not only climax the gospel stories, but invite us to study how the activity of this Risen Lord relates to what the earthly Jesus did in his ministry.

1

1 Corinthians 15:3-11
"An Apologetic Resurrection Story"

The material on the resurrection of Jesus in 1 Cor 15:3-11 has always enjoyed a special place in the New Testament because scholars judge it to be the oldest literary reference to Jesus' resurrection as well as one of the most comprehensive comments about it. Paul begins his account of Jesus' resurrection by reminding his listeners of the sacred, traditional character of his remarks, "I hand on to you ... what I received" (15:3). Scholars generally remind us that Paul's account of the Eucharist in 1 Cor 11 begins the same way, thus reinforcing the reader's sense of the importance of this material.

1 Cor 11:23 (Eucharist)	*1 Cor 15:3 (Resurrection)*
For I **received** from the Lord what I also **handed** on to you	For I **hand on** to you what I also **received**

"Receiving" and "handing on," moreover, are key elements in the transmission of sacred traditions in ancient Judaism, a terminological point about which Paul the Pharisee would be familiar. The point is, Paul is quite conscious of the sacredness of the formula (15:3b-4) which is the foundation of his faith and preaching, for its introduction with this

remark about "receiving" and "handing on" serves as a
drum roll to call attention to what follows.

Structure & Form

The passage under consideration (15:3-11) consists of
three parts, each with a distinct shape and function:
A. 15:3b-4 confessional formula of
        Jesus' death & resurrection
B. 15:5-8 list of those to whom
        the risen Jesus appeared
C. 15:9-11 apologia for Paul's ministry
If we are to appreciate all of the nuances and information
encoded in these three parts, we should look at each of them
more closely from a critical, inquiring viewpoint.

15:3b-4 This summary statement about Jesus' death and
resurrection is cast in a parallel form which is usually reserved for sacred formulae which needed to be easily
remembered, such as liturgical or confessional formulae.

1. Christ died	1. he was raised
for our sins	on the third day
2. in accordance	2. in accordance
with the Scriptures	with the Scriptures
3. and was buried	3. and he appeared to...

Scholars argue that this sacred formula antedates the writing
of 1 Corinthians by many years, and probably goes back to
a primitive confessional formula of a church already en-
gaged in a mission to the Gentiles, Antioch perhaps. Its
completeness, then, is all the more striking for its antiquity.
Jesus' death is treated kerygmatically and apologetically: he
died "for our sins" and his death is in accord with God's
providential plan as revealed in the Hebrew Scriptures.
Proof that Jesus really died is provided in the note that "he
was buried"—that is, he was removed from the land of the
living and placed in the realm of the dead, that is, in a tomb.

Balancing the remark about Jesus' death, the second half of the formula proclaims that Jesus "was raised" by God, whose resurrection also has a positive as well as an apologetic note. As we shall shortly see, the manifestation of the Risen Jesus was perceived from a "soteriological" perspective, that is, it was evaluated as beneficial to Jesus' followers, for it commissioned leaders to guide the followers of Jesus. And like his death, it was in accord with God's plan in the Scriptures. Furthermore, just as Jesus' "burial" functioned as proof that he was truly dead, so his "appearances" to Cephas and the others function as proof that he is back in the land of the living. The sacred formula has joined together confession of Jesus' death *and* resurrection, giving them comparable importance and talking about them in parallel terms. Death and the undoing of death constitute the core of the kerygma.

15:5-6 It is important to note that these verses contain an unadorned list of those to whom Jesus manifested himself. We are told no details whatever about time or place, only a bare list of names of those to whom Jesus manifested himself, a point that has a bearing on how we appreciate the very detailed accounts of the appearances of the Risen Jesus in the Gospels. As form critics have shown apropos of Jesus' miracles, his passion and even his resurrection, at first in the early church there was only a list, a bare summary of events or information. For example, in the early source called "Q," there is only the barest catalogue of Jesus' miracles with no narrative details: "The blind receive their sight, the lame walk, lepers are cleansed, the deaf hear and the dead are raised" (Lk 7:22//Mt 11:5), a list which was narrated in great detail much later by the evangelists. Before Mark put the story of Jesus' Passion into full narrative form, a brief summary of events seems to have sufficed, "he was handed over, condemned, crucified and died" (see 1 Cor 11:23). So too with Jesus' resurrection, the early church at first possessed only a terse list of those to whom Jesus manifested himself, a list which would in time be fleshed out with full narrative and dramatic details by Luke, Matthew and John.

The list, however, is not without shape and formal content. Scholars indicate that the list of people mentioned in 15:5-6 is really *two* lists, which are carefully cast in parallel form.

List One	List Two
1. Cephas	1. James
2. the Twelve	2. all the apostles
3. more than 500	3. Paul

When we identify the persons referred to in the lists, we begin to get a sense of the shape and function of the two groups. "Cephas," of course, is Simon Peter, whom Jesus commissioned first (Jn 1:42; Lk 5:10) and made chief shepherd of the early church (see Jn 21:15-17). There is only the barest mention of the tradition of Jesus' special appearance to Peter in Lk 24:34, although Jn 21 seems to be intent on expanding that terse reference into a full narrative. "The Twelve" are the apostles whom Jesus gathered around him during his ministry (Mk 3:13-19) and whom he commissioned to preach (Lk 24:47-49; Acts 1:15-26). "More than 500 Brethren" remains an obscure reference for us.

Turning to the second list, we reckon that "James" is not the brother of Zebedee (Mk 1:19-20) of whom Acts 12:1-2 records a martyr's death in the early days of the Jerusalem church. This "James" is probably the James of Acts 12:17; 15:13-21 and Gal 2:9, the second leader of the church at Jerusalem. "All the apostles" are surely not "the Twelve" just mentioned, but other commissioned preachers (see Rom 16:7). Finally, we recognize "Paul," the apostolic preacher to whom Jesus appeared, "Am I not an apostle? Have I not seen the Lord" (1 Cor 9:1).

Looking carfully at the two lists, we sense that "Cephas" and "the Twelve" represent those commissioned to preach to Jews, the House of Israel, whereas "James" represents the figure authorized to conduct the mission to the Gentiles (Acts 15:13-21), which was carried out by "all the apostles," to say nothing of Paul, the great apostle to the Gentiles. The two lists, then, represent the two foci of ministry in the early church, those whose field of endeavor was primarily Jews and those whose apostolate was basically to the Gentiles, a distinction mentioned by Paul as a result of his visit to the Jerusalem church, "James and Cephas and John gave to me and Barnabas the right hand of fellowship, that we should go to the Gentiles and they to the Circumcised" (Gal 2:9).

But even as we recognize that two equal, parallel directions for the preaching of the early church are outlined in the list, we gain a critical insight into the *function* of the manifestations of Jesus to these persons. The Risen Jesus commissions them. The stories of Jesus' resurrection manifestations function as the commissioning of those to whom he appeared. Those who believe in Jesus in the early church, then, are gifted with the presence of clearly identified leaders and preachers, whose leadership is legitimate and trustworthy and whose preaching is based on eye-witness experience of the Risen Lord. The foundation of the covenant community gathered in Jesus' name and memory rests on a most solid foundation (see Eph 2:20; 2 Peter 1:19-21).

15:8-11 After the terse list, Paul spends considerable time explaining his place in the list. He admits that he is the runt of the litter, "one untimely born," "the least," and one who does not deserve to be ranked with the other apostles, "because I persecuted the church of God." Balancing these disqualifications he affirms, however, that "by the grace of God I am what I am." God's sovereign freedom and power, of course, are unquestionable, and if it pleases God to choose the likes of Paul, so be it. One cannot but help hear in these remarks a strong apologetic note, to which we will return shortly.

The investigation of the structure and form of 15:3-11 has produced important clues as to its meaning. And we are duly awed in the presence of these ancient traditions. But the importance of the past can only be felt in the present when we ask a new question of this text: what is the purpose and function of Paul's account of this material vis-à-vis this particular church at Corinth? Of all of his letters, why does

Paul speak *this* way to *this* church? Even a casual reading of
1 Cor 15 indicates that there are many questions in the
Corinthian church about "resurrection."
1. "How can some of you say, 'There is no
        resurrection of the dead?'" (15:12)
2. "Some will ask, 'How are the dead raised?
        With what kind of body do they come?'" (15:35).
Time does not allow us to survey the many issues and
questions raised in 1 Cor 15 about "the resurrection," either
Jesus' or that of Christian dead, even our own. But from the
special language used ("receive...hand on"), the length of
the arguments, the extended Adam-Jesus comparison (15:21-
23, 42-49) and the appeal to special sources ("scripture" 15:4;
special revelation in 15:51), Paul felt the need to speak at
great length and with considerable force about the resurrection. Let us look more closely at how 15:3-11 functions
vis-à-vis the situation at Corinth.

Background

The full flavor of Paul's remarks in 15:3-11 depends on
our appreciation of the church to whom Paul sent this
letter. The first information we get about it is Paul's appeal
"that there be no dissensions among you" (1:10), for the fact
of the matter is that Corinth is a quarreling community split
into factions: "Each one of you says, 'I belong to Paul,' or 'I
belong to Apollos,' or 'I belong to Cephas'" (1:12; see 3:3
and 11:18-19). Although we know of fights and disagree-
ments in other Pauline churches (see Phil 4:2 and even 2
Cor 10-11), the problems in Corinth are not just competing
tensions between individuals, but clashes of theology and
disputes over ideology among the members of the church.
We can overhear the conversation at Corinth only through
Paul's letter, which may give us a biased view, but it remains
our only access to this material. As Paul sees it, there are
not just factions but different values which divide the group.

It is interesting to note how even Paul describes the people and situations of this church in dualistic language which accentuates their factions and divisions: there are "wise" as well as "foolish" (1:27; 3:18), "strong" as well as "weak" (1:27b; 2:1-5); "spiritual" as well as "fleshly" (2:13-14; 3:1-3); "adults" and "babes" (3:1-3); those "in the know" and those "*not* in the know" (8:1, 10-11); and "free" and "unfree" (8:9; 10:29). Even the body is divided into "eye" or "ear," "head" or "foot" (12:16, 21), into "honorable" and "unpresentable" parts (12:23), and "greater" and "inferior" members (12:24). The church, then, is radically divided.

Gathering diverse pieces of information in the letter, we can hypothetically reconstruct a certain point of view which Paul considers defective and in need of qualification. The chief problem according to Paul lies with the group who are described as "wise," "strong," "spiritual" etc. What do they think and why do they think such thoughts? Reconstructing their theology from Paul's meager data, we guess that they might be said to hold the following views:

> 1. They focus on Jesus' **resurrection** as the pivotal event which liberated Jesus (and his followers) from all limits: Jesus cannot die again; he is beyond the limits of the physical body; he is radically "free" from all earthly laws and rules. As Jesus, so also with those who share his resurrection.
>
> 2. They are **pneumatic** or spiritual Christians, who have received the Spirit powerfully and lastingly at baptism, which means eating spiritual food and drinking spiritual drink (10:1-4).
>
> 3. In virtue of this Spirit, they gain great **wisdom**: knowledge, insight, mysteries, and revelations which sometimes transcend the words and teachings of the earthly Jesus.
>
> 4. With Spirit comes radical **freedom**. When the Spirit is present, it is "Lord" (2 Cor 3:18), in the sense that in the Spirit one is "subject" to a higher power or law, not to earthly considerations, authorities or laws.
>
> 5. With the Spirit comes **power**, or the demonstration

that one is beyond the limits of body and flesh.

6. Such spiritual people believe that the final victory of Jesus over sin, death and all things earthly is **already achieved** in their baptism, the gift of Spirit and the present sharing of the status of the Risen Jesus.

It would seem, then, that certain "pneumatics" at Corinth would tend to place all value in what is associated with the reception of Spirit and the status which flows from having it. Since Spirit is linked with Jesus' resurrection, not his death, resurrection is linked with freedom, power, and knowledge, all of which are the present possession of the elite at Corinth.

What would this look like structurally? What would the social dynamics of such a group be like? All value is being placed in things "spiritual," rather than things material, which would lead these "pneumatics" first of all to have a christology quite different than that preached in the early church. Celebrating spirit and power, they would find little of value or importance in the cross of Christ, which Paul admits is "weakness and foolishness" (1:18-25). According to Paul's preaching, the cross is expiation for our sins (Rom 3:25), justification of past trespasses (Rom 4:25); by his supreme obedience to God even unto death, Jesus undid the disobedience of Adam (Rom 5:18-19), gaining acquittal for all. But this would not be valued by people who find no value in body and flesh, much less pain and suffering. Furthermore, already victorious with the Risen Jesus, they have no expectation of his return to judge; for they have already crossed from death to life, from this world to the world to come. So strong a view of Jesus' resurrection, then, can tend to devalue the meaning of Jesus' cross and his future coming.

In terms of church structure and dynamics, when value is put only on what is spiritual, there is a corresponding devaluation of certain aspects of church life and practice. With the stress on resurrected newness and with the experience of the spirit of freedom, there tends to be a devaluation of tradition and of what the earthly Jesus handed on to his followers. In its place, the Spirit inspires new mysteries and prophecies in those possessed, which lead them into a future untrammeled by past norms, practices or traditions. When led by the Spirit, "pneumatics" are truly freed from the Old Testament Law and all laws, which apply to those who are either still in the flesh or not yet freed from slavery to sin and death. Pneumatics, moreover, need not bother about what they do in the flesh, for they are truly beyond the body, which is now neutral or morally irrelevant. Finally, truly spiritual people who are genuinely free owe obedience only to the Spirit, not to any person invested with role or status in the group; for they *know* without being taught and they can *decide for themselves* without direction from another, certainly not from one who is *not* spiritual. In general, they tend to be strong individualists who, because free in the Spirit, are neither bound by concerns of scandal to weak members nor normed by directions of practical charity to others. When seen in this special context, the "resurrection" becomes a symbol for some of a christology which celebrates the present transcendence of limit, flesh and human structure. It represents a value which authorizes a certain individualism, a radically future orientation to life and a transcendence of authority, norms, laws, and rules.

Function

It was to such a faction in the Corinthian church that Paul addressed 15:3-11, and it helps us to grasp the nuances of Paul's argument if we can indicate how he is coping with genuine church problems in the way he phrases and uses the materials expressed there. For example, to those who because of spiritual inspiration claim to be privy to mysteries and secrets, Paul insists that tradition still counts. Hence he insists that his preaching of Jesus' cross and resurrection constitutes what he "received" and "handed on," a norm of faith which is applicable to all Christians. It is not accidental, then, that Paul would hand on the whole tradition at this point about Jesus' resurrection *and cross,* for together they make up the fullness of the mystery of Jesus.

To the elite who considered themselves free, especially from authority as this is localized in humans who might not be as strong or eloquent as themselves, Paul is pleased to present the official list of those to whom Jesus manifested himself. Although these "pneumatics" celebrated the Risen Jesus, the fact that according to 15:5-8 this same Risen Lord commissioned specific people to preach and teach simply must be taken into account by the whole church, especially the elite. The Risen Jesus authorized certain persons and so "authority" has a legitimate place among Jesus' followers. It should be noted that apropos of genuine "spiritual" gifts, Paul indicates those truly led by the Spirit will make a confession of Jesus which includes an affirmation of authority and obedience, "No one can say 'Jesus is Lord' except by the Spirit" (12:3). And apropos of the Risen Lord himself, Paul notes that Jesus, even in his risen state when God shall put all things under his feet, is himself still "subjected" to God, "When all things are subjected to him (Jesus), then the Son himself will also be subjected to him (God) who put all things under him" (15:28). As God has authorized the Risen Jesus, so the Lord commissions and legitimates others for ministry in the church. In response to the pneumatic elites, Paul insists that the Risen Jesus does *not* symbolize total freedom or lack of authority.

In a very apologetic manner Paul gathers the negative things which are said about him in the Corinthian church. He is the runt of the litter, "last," "least," "unworthy to be an apostle" because he persecuted the church (15:8-9). Throughout this letter Paul has alluded to slurs about him as an unenlightened, uncharismatic, non-powerful person who gives his flock milk, not solid food (3:1). The remarks in 15:8-9, then, are dealing with the overall pattern of the penumatics' perception of Paul. In the face of so much disqualification, Paul celebrates the sovereign freedom of

God: "I am what I am by the grace of God" (15:10). Nor has God's grace been un-powerful or un-productive, for Paul actually boasts that he has "worked harder than any of them" (15:10b). An unlikely choice for God's favor, Paul is legitimated and commissioned to preach as well as to administer this church. And so, in one sense, Paul claims to be as charismatic as any of the pneumatics, for God has graced him and the Risen Lord has appeared to him and commissioned him.

Conclusion

While 15:3-11 basically repeats the venerable tradition of the early church about the Risen Jesus, Paul is not merely repeating that tradition for its own sake. He is positively using it as a corrective apologetic argument in his conflict with the pneumatics in Corinth. To their claims to be unbound and unnormed by traditions of the past, Paul reminds them that the doctrine of the Risen Jesus which he preaches is the genuine "gospel" which they once gladly received as true and so were saved by it (15:1-2). Tradition has a legitimate role to play in the preaching and teaching of the church. To their claims to be free and not under human authority, Paul reminds the church of the figures whom the Risen Jesus commissioned for teaching and preaching, thus legitimating their role and status in the early church. Even in the cosmos inaugurated by Jesus' resurrection, there remains a valid place for authority and legitimate roles and statuses in the church of the Risen One. Finally, in response to the personal slurs about Paul's non-pneumatic behavior and status, Paul reminds his hearers of the heavenly grace given him by God, a grace admittedly surprising and unusual, but a grace with legitimates Paul vis-à-vis the church at Corinth. The remarks about the Risen Jesus in 15:3-11, then, must be savored in terms of their apologetic function if we are to listen to Paul's pastoral preaching to his church. The resurrection stories were no abstract idea for him, but a vital truth which gives value and shape to the Body of Christ. They seem to have less to say about the remote future and more about contemporary life in the company of Jesus and his saints.

2

Matthew 28:16-20
"Sovereign of the Universe"

Turning to the Gospels, we would like to begin with Mark's story of Jesus' resurrection, because that gospel is considered to be the oldest and so the major source used by both Matthew and Luke. But the original version of Mark has no story of Jesus' resurrection appearance, a point which greatly puzzles scholars. Some time after Mark finished his gospel, a later editor appended a resurrection story (16:9-20), which appears to be merely a compendium of pieces of information from the other gospels and Acts of the Apostles. Since that passage in Mark is not original to his gospel but is a derivative of other gospels, there is no particular need to study it here. But in Matthew, who wrote shortly after Mark and who used Mark's gospel extensively in his own account, we find a remarkable appearance of Jesus at the very end of the gospel which climaxes Matthew's presentation of him as God's authentic Son and Lord of the covenant community. What Mark does not narrate, Matthew does, and so we turn there.

Structure and Form

Every good story starts out with some indication of time and place, "Once upon a time...," and the account in Mt

28:16-20 is no exception. First we note the setting of the encounter with Jesus in "Galilee, the mountain to which Jesus had directed them" (28:16). The evangelist wants the reader to link 28:16 with 26:32, where Jesus predicted that after his passion he would gather his flock again as a good shepherd, "After I am raised up, I will go before you to Galilee." 28:16, then, suggests that the "shepherd who was struck" (26:31) and whose ruin caused the sheep to scatter returns vindicated and powerful to resume his role as shepherd and royal leader. And the very gathering of the disciples in Galilee on the mountain suggests a band of followers obedient to Jesus' word. A prophecy, moreover, is fulfilled, indicating Jesus' providential control of history.

The significance of the details of this account of Jesus' appearance can be appreciated when we take note of the literary form which seems to structure the narrative. There is a rather common literary form found in both the Hebrew and Christian Scriptures which is used to describe the vocation of a great patriarch or prophet to be leader of God's covenant community. When it is found in its full form, this vocation commissioning has five points (see Chart): 1) *introduction* and setting, 2) *confrontation:* a heavenly messenger meets the one chosen for leadership, a meeting which provokes a fearful reaction which is calmed by a word of reassurance, such as "Do not be afraid"; 3) then the messenger delivers the *commission,* 4) to which the one being chosen frequently *objects,* which requires the messenger to *reassure* him and offer a *sign* of proof or confirmation, 5) at the *conclusion* of which, the messenger departs. As chart one indicates, the form is clearly the structure of the vocation stories of Moses, Gideon and Jeremiah, but also seems to describe the call or vocation to leadership of Jesus' disciples for the ministry of preaching the gospel about the Risen Lord.

Reading Mt 28:16-20 in the light of this common vocation form, we note the following:

FORM	Exodus	Judges	Jeremiah	Matthew	Luke	John 20	John 21
1. Introduction	3:13	6:11	1:1-3	28:16a	24:33-36a	20:19a	21:1-6
2. Confrontation	3:4-6a	6:12	1:4	28:17a	24:36b	20:19b	21:7-14
Reaction	3:6b	6:13	---	28:17b	24:37	20:20	21:12
Reassurance	3:7-9	---	1:5a	28:18a	24:38-40		---
3. Commission	3:10, 16-18	6:14	1:5b	28:18b-20a	24:44-48	20:21-23	21:15-17, 18-19
4. Objection	4:1, 10, 13	6:15	1:6	---	---	20:25	---
Reassurance	4:11-12	6:16	1:7-8	28:20b	24:49	20:26	
Sign	4:2-4, 6-7, 8-9	6:17, 36ff	1:9-10		---	20:27	
5. Conclusion	---	---	---		24:50-53	---	---

1. Norman Habel, "The Form and Significance of the Call Narratives," ZAW 77 (1965) 297-323.
2. Benjamin Hubbard, The Matthean Redaction of a Primitive Apostolic Commissioning.

1) *introduction* (28:16): the disciples are gathered on a mountain in Galilee at the word of Jesus;

2) *confrontation* (28:17a): Jesus appears to them and they perceive him; but like many vocations, there is an ambivalent *reaction* to this appearance, not uncommon to prophets and leaders: "they worshiped him, but some doubted" (28:17b); this prompts a *reassurance* on the part of Jesus, "And Jesus came to them and said, 'All authority in heaven and on earth has been given to me'" (28:18);

3) *commission* (28:19): Jesus then gets to the point of this event; he commissions the disciples as his legitimate spokesmen and as leaders of the covenant community of his followers: "Go and make disciples of all nations, baptizing them in the name of the Father and of the Son and of the Holy Spirit";

4) there is no *objection* to this commission, as there is elsewhere, but a final *reassurance* is given which resembles the same reassurance given Israel's prophets and judges: "Behold, I am with you always, to the close of the age" (see Jdg 6:16; Jer 1:8).

The value of recognizing this form in Mt 28:16-20 lies in the immediate focus it gives to the narrative: Jesus' appearance functions as a *commissioning,* the establishment of legitimate authority in Jesus' covenant community. This commissioning confirms the gathering of Jesus' apostles (see Mt 10:1-5), thus establishing a continuity between the deeds of the earthly Jesus and those of the Risen Lord.

Yet if the form identifies the commissioning of the disciples in 28:19-20a as the focus of the story, there is a remarkable unity to the passage which also focuses on Jesus. One needs to keep tabs on the adjective "all," which appears frequently in the narrative and serves as a unifying theme in the passage:

All authority in heaven and earth has been given to me...

Make disciples of *all* nations...
Teaching them to observe *all* that I have commanded
you...
Behold, I am with you *all* days.

This is no accidental phenomenon, for the evangelist wants
to depict Jesus as the sovereign Lord appointed by God
with complete authority in the heavenly and earthly realms—
no mean position. All the scope of his sovereignty is not
limited to Israel (see 10:5-6), but extends to all peoples on
earth. The commissioned disciples, moreover, must teach
the fullness of Jesus' message (*all* that I command you), just
as Jesus himself did not discard one iota or a dot from
God's law (5:18). And his rule is for all times, to the close of
the age. All authority over all peoples concerning all aspects
of their lives for all times. The obscure carpenter from
Galilee has been transformed into the Sovereign of the
world. The structure and form of 28:16-20, then, clearly
point to a story of authority (Jesus') and legitimation (the
disciples') for all peoples for all times.

Background

The forcefulness of Matthew's narrative here is further
enhanced when we note how the evangelist purposely alludes
to a biblical story of power and vindication. In Daniel, we
read of a figure called the "Son of Man," who is generally
considered to stand for God's loyal, persecuted followers in
Israel about the time of the Maccabean wars. Rejected by
many on earth and even martyred, they are surprisingly
vindicated by God in heaven, who reverses their lowly
status and gives them glory and dominion. Like the other
evangelists, at Jesus' trial Matthew equates him with this
"Son of Man." When rejected on earth by the Sanhedrin,
Jesus predicts his future vindication by God in heaven,
"You will see the 'Son of Man' seated at the right hand of
the Power" (26:64). It is one thing to predict vindication,

and quite another thing to reflect on its fulfillment, which is just what 28:16-20 narrates. Matthew apparently used the sacred text of Dan 7:14, which describes the ultimate vindication of the Son of Man, as the content of Jesus' remarks to the apostles, as the following synopsis suggests.

Prophecy (Dan 7:14)	*Fulfillment (Mt 28:19)*
1. And to him was given dominion & glory &	1. All authority in heaven and on earth has been given to me
2. that all peoples, nations and languages should serve him;	2. Go, make disciples of all nations
3. his dominion is an everlasting dominion, which shall not pass away; and his kingdom is one that shall not be destroyed.	3. I am with you always, to the close of the age.

We are only speculating, but there are many reasons why Matthew would tend to draw a parallel between Jesus and the Son of Man. First, both tell the story of a vindicted martyr, a person faithful to God but rejected on earth, whom God vindicated and exalted in heaven. A pattern is confirmed by this vindication which Jesus noted all through his teaching, viz., how the righteous suffer on earth (see 5:10-12), but are rewarded in God's heavenly kingdom. There is a tradition, in fact, that all of God's holy prophets were rejected on earth, even martyred (23:37). One's suffering on earth does *not* mean that God is displeased with the sufferer or that such a person is a sinner receiving an appropriate punishment; on the contrary, God's saints and prophets all were rejected. And so an apologetic note is sounded in Jesus' defense. Second, Matthew frequently affirms Jesus' legitimacy by noting how his words or actions fulfil a prophecy of God in the Scriptures (see 1:22-23; 2:5-6; 8:17 etc.) Jesus is no recent interloper, but the one whose destiny God foreknew and foreordained in the prophecies of Scripture. And so the allusion to Dan 7:14 in Mt 28:19

sounds another apologetic note. Finally, although the infant Jesus was proclaimed King of the Jews, it remains for us to learn that he actually assumed his throne and reigned. The account in 28:19 indeed proclaims that the one heralded as Ruler and Sovereign at his birth finally assumed his reign, which will never end.

Redaction

Although we know that the evangelists handed on many ancient traditions about Jesus, they were skillful in adapting the preaching about Jesus to the situations of their churches. And so it is a very profitable task to note how typical Matthew's account of Jesus' appearance is, how it reflects many of his characteristic ways of thinking and expressing himself vis-à-vis his own community for whom he wrote. Let us take note of the themes, words and motifs characteristic of this evangelist, which make up the fabric of 28:16-20.

A Mountain. Matthew frequently indicates that significant events in salvation history take place on mountains. For example, mountains are places of revelation. At the beginning of his career Jesus ascended a mountain from which he gave a new Law to his disciples (5:1); and later in his career, Jesus revealed from a mountain the future ruin of Jerusalem and the end of the world (24:3ff). Mountains are places of prayer (14:23), even of commissioning (17:1ff). How appropriate, then, that Jesus would appear one last time on "a mountain" both to reveal and to commission.

In Galilee. Apart from indicating fulfillment of Jesus' word to go to Galilee (26:32), the notice that the mountain was in "Galilee" reminds us of the very beginning of Jesus' ministry at which point the evangelist noted that "Galilee" was a special, even a symbolic place according to Isa 9:1-2. Mt 4:12-16 is a passage which, because of its position at the very beginning of Jesus' mission, has a symbolic significance for the whole of his ministry; it constitutes a programmatic statement for the theological geography of Jesus' mission as well as for the scope of the audience to whom Jesus will go. "Galilee" in 4:12-16 is interpreted according to Isa 9:1-2, which gives it an authoritative meaning based on God's holy word. In 4:12-16//Isa 9:1-2, "Galilee" is "Galilee of *the Gentiles*" which reminds us of "all nations" in 28:19; it was a place of "darkness" for which Jesus provides the light of his teaching (28:20); and it was "in the region and shadow of death," in response to which Jesus proclaims baptism unto life (28:19c). "Galilee" in 4:12-16 and 28:16, then, is a place symbolic of the universal mission of Jesus and his offering of light and life to all peoples.

Worshiped Him. This term means not so much adoration of Jesus as God as a posture of profound respect. One thinks of the deep bows given at court to sovereigns, even the Arabic salaam. Matthew noted that Jesus always received such response as his due, either as an infant reverenced by Magi (2:11) or as a prophet besought by a leper (8:1) or as the powerful "Son of God" (14:33). This appears to be a typical Semitic way of saying that Jesus always was an honorable person in his culture.

All Nations. There was a time when Jesus' early followers were rather sectarian, perceiving that Jesus was sent "only to the lost sheep of the house of Israel" (10:5-6; 15:24). But in time, the early church came to see that God intended the revelation in Jesus for all peoples, Jews and Gentiles alike (see Mt 15:21-28). And so, Matthew indicates both at the beginning and the end of his account of Jesus' ministry this universal scope of Jesus' words and teachings. It is no accident that God draws pagan Magi by star, by dream and by Scripture to find and reverence Jesus. Comparably, in 28:19 Jesus himself commissions a universal mission without ethnic distinction, a mission already heralded in the account of messengers who went to the thoroughfares and gathered "all whom they found, both bad and good" into the king's banquet (22:9-10).

Teaching Them to Observe All that I Have Commanded You. The gospel tradition, while it portrays Jesus as a healing prophet, also indicates how Jesus functioned as a teaching prophet who handed on a reformed word of God. Jesus may no longer endorse circumcision, require strict sabbath observance and the like, but he was no anti-authority teacher who discarded the will of God so clearly contained in Israel's Scriptures. According to Matthew, Jesus taught a reformed Torah, a purified way of serving God both in deed and in spirit (see the "Antitheses" in 5:21-46). As authorized by God, Jesus' words become the new Torah, the new scripture, the authentic way of life for God's covenant.

I Am with You. Although we noted earlier that this phrase is best understood as a formal element of *reassurance,* Matthew also notes in 1:23 that Jesus is prophesied to be "Emmanuel," that is, the proof and means of God's abiding presence with the covenant people, for "Emmanuel" literally means "God with us." For it is an ancient tradition in Israel that God's word is not far off but near and present (see Deut 30:11-14). Indeed, the temple is no longer the locus of God's presence to the covenant community, especially since it has been destroyed in war by the time Matthew wrote. All the more important, then, is the note that God has not abandoned his people nor do they lack a locus where to meet God. Jesus, who is present always with them, is that sacred "place" even if they are scattered on mission throughout the world. God remains always near and present, even as Jesus is always present to the church.

It is easy to see that Matthew's version of the resurrection appearance fully harmonizes with the way in which he tells the rest of the gospel story. This suggests that the narrative details in 28:16-20 probably do not stem from a purely historical inquiry on Matthew's part as from his concern to show the continuity of Jesus' ministry, both in his earthly ministry and in his risen state.

Christology

The most important places in sermons, speeches and stories tend to be the beginnings and endings. And Matthew is no exception, for the Infancy Narratives tell a remarkable story about Jesus as Son of Abraham, Son of David and Son of God. The conclusion of the gospel likewise compresses in a few verses most of the exciting and remarkable things Matthew has to say about Jesus. According to the parallel with Dan 7:14, Jesus is the righteous servant of God who was martyred on earth, but vindicated and enthroned by God in heaven. And according to the form of a commission story which underlies 28:16-20, Jesus functions as a figure of supreme authority who appoints ministers to do his bidding throughout the world. He is the ultimate patriarch of God's covenant people, their consummate prophet and their eternal sovereign. No specific title is mentioned about the Risen Jesus here, but the scope of his authority and the manner in which he acts clearly indicate that this risen Jesus is Lord of the universe. And so, his resurrection is not merely his vindication (Dan 7:14) but also his enthronement as ruler of God's people. He truly is at God's right hand.

Ecclesiology

As well as the narrative speaks about Jesus, it also has much to say about his followers and the covenant community which depended on this narrative for its charter and identity. The Risen Jesus formally proclaims a universal mission to all peoples of the world, a dramatic shift in the perspective of the early followers of Jesus. God's covenant community continues the covenant relationship God made with Abraham and David, a covenant based on God's promise and one which was at odds with the norms and values of its culture. Ancient groups tended to be tightly bounded and guarded against "foreigners" or outsiders;

even Israel tended to speak of itself as God's "chosen people," distinguishing itself as a holy nation set apart from the pagan peoples among whom Israel lived. In such groups, there were rules of hierarchy and rank, whereby value and favor rested on first-born males, etc. But in the covenant with Abraham and David, all such notions of rank, hierarchy and separateness were transcended, at least temporarily; for, in Abraham, God chose a non-Israelite and in David, the youngest son of Jesse—both choices out of the ordinary. In the accounts of God's dealings with Abraham and David a principle came to be established that God could act freely and choose the outsider over the insider, the youngest over the eldest son. If one wanted, one could trace this pattern through the Hebrew Scriptures, noting God's favor to Abel over Cain, to Isaac over Ishmael, to Jacob over his brothers, to David over his brothers, and to Solomon over his siblings (see also Rom 9:6-13). A certain inclusiveness and universalism is encoded in this biblical model of covenant and the symbolic stories of Abraham and David. The gospel of Matthew begins with the proclamation that Jesus is "Son of Abraham, Son of David" (1:1-16), a proclamation which signals that the pattern of God's dealings with these two national heroes is operative once more in Jesus. Grace and favor will be shown outside the fixed, traditional lines of Jewish life; an initial note of inclusiveness is sounded. And when the gospel ends with Jesus sending his disciples to make converts of "all nations," the note of inclusiveness and universality heralded in God's covenant with Abraham and David is made explicit. The gospel, then, begins and ends with a proclamation of a universal covenant community in which Magi and Jerusalem Jews (2:1-11) as well as Jesus' Jewish disciples and Gentiles are included (28:16-20).

In his ministry in Galilee, Jesus called, gathered and commissioned "twelve disciples" to preach, teach and heal in his name (10:1-4). As important as that commission was, it remained to be confirmed and elevated by the final commissioning of the disciples by the Risen Jesus in 28:16-

20. At stake here are issues of authority and legitimacy among the leaders of the early churches, issues which perhaps are not important to us, but which were vital to the survival and direction of the early church. Of course, not every follower of Jesus became an authorized leader or a legitimated teacher. And in time, there was even conflict and rivalry between leaders who knew the historical Jesus (see Acts 1:21-22; 1 Jn 1:1-4) and others whose claim to leadership rested on charismatic achievements, such as miracles, prophecy and the like (see 2 Cor 10-11). How to settle the issue? Criteria for authority and legitimacy can come from two directions: a) *ascribed* leadership (a person appointed by a higher authority, such as a provincial governor; a person born to be king, such as the royal heir) and b) *achieved* leadership (a person who, because of his deeds and benefactions, is acclaimed hero and leader). According to 10:1-4, Jesus' disciples are "ascribed" leaders of his covenant community, a valid and strong claim for leadership. But that claim was strengthened in the face of rival claims by the narrative in 28:16-20, whereby their leadership is also "achieved" leadership based on revelations and christophanies. The disciples in 28:16-20 are treated much the way the figure of Peter is dealt with in this gospel. His leadership status is traditionally based on Jesus' "ascribing" premier status to him as Fisher of Men (4:18-19; 10:2). But in Matthew's version of Peter's legitimation, he is also qualified because of his "achievements": 1) he has revelations (16:17; 17:1-8) and 2) he performs remarkable deeds, such as walking on water (14:28-29) and mysteriously finding a tax coin in a fish's mouth (17:24-27). In 28:16-20, all of the disciples, as well as Peter, are credited with valid leadership which is both *ascribed* by Jesus and *achieved* through visions and revelations of the Risen Lord. The church of Matthew, then, is solidly grounded on the rock of the Apostles. Such is the task of the Risen Jesus, to found his church (16:18).

The Risen Jesus graciously endows his covenant community with the gift of his teaching, his Torah. In the ancient world, the goodness of a people was recognized in the richness and solidity of its laws, its way of life. Conversely, the worst accusation that could be made against a people was that they were lawless antinomians, who respected neither God's law or the laws which made city and nation life possible and enjoyable. Jesus, for all of his attacks on the Torah of the Pharisees, was a reformer of Torah, not its destroyer. He was no lawless person nor an advocate of lawlessness. As the Risen Lord of God's covenant community, he ordains the best of laws for his followers, "Teach them to observe all that I have commanded you."

Not only does the Risen Jesus declare an inclusive community with stable leadership, he mandates a wise way of life for them. In these regards, moreover, the Risen Jesus continues his ministry. For he is no absent sovereign, but one who is "with you all days, to the close of the age," and who continues to act as a Davidic Shepherd in gathering all sheep into his one flock where they can prosper by living according to his gift of Torah. Mt 28:16-20, then, tells a powerful story of the ongoing ministry of the Lord Jesus vis-a-vis a covenant community which is both inclusive and graced. It is, moreover, a stable community with clear lines of authority and a clear rule of life.

3

Luke 24:13-35
"The Risen Shepherd"

The gospel of Luke narrates that Jesus appeared to a variety of people on that first Easter day. In what is only a passing, but important note, Luke records that "he appeared to Simon" (24:34), although this appearance is never narrated. Rather the evangelist tells in great detail of manifestations by Jesus, first to disciples who had lost faith and left the group of Jesus' disciples (24:13-35), and then to disciples still gathered together, but quite uncertain about Jesus (24:36-49). The first story, which is unique to Luke, appears nowhere else in the New Testament, whereas the second resurrection story resembles the great commissioning scene found at the end of Matthew and John. Both appearances, however, basically tell a gospel story about Jesus' continued ministry even on that Easter day.

Structure

Forceful and important narratives often have remarkable structures which clarify important aspects in them, even as they focus on key elements in them. Lk 24:13-35 is no exception. One can observe how this long and seemingly complicated narrative is immediately clarified by the chiastic form in which it is cast. "Chiasm," a very common literary form in Greco-Roman and Semitic literature, refers to the "X" shape or symmetrical arrangement of parts whereby the end resembles the beginning. Lk 24:13-35 exemplifies this form:

A. Journey from Jerusalem (24:12)
   B. " ...talking about all these things which happened" (24:15)
      C. Jesus appears (24:15)
         D. The disciples' eyes are closed (24:16)
            E. Jesus takes the initiative and teaches (24:17-27)
            E'. Jesus takes the initiative and feeds (24:28-30)
         D'. Their eyes are opened (24:31a)
      C'. Jesus disappears (24:31b)
   B'. " ... he talked with us on the road" (24:32)
A'. Journey back to Jerusalem (24:33)

This type of structural analysis offers significant clues to the meaning of the narrative, for it automatically highlights the central part of the story where Jesus takes the pastoral initiative to teach and feed (E & E'). The paralleling of events, moreover, indicates that a dynamic process is at work, how the disciples move away from Jerusalem in despair but return in faith and how they change from people whose hearts were cold and whose eyes were blinded to true followers of Jesus whose hearts "burn on the way" and whose eyes are opened. All of these observations, more-over, point to the on-going ministry of the Risen Jesus as the focus of the story, a remarkable piece of good news for Luke's church.

Form

Although Lk 24:13-35 is not cast in the form of a vocation commissioning, as was Mt 28:16-20, there are certain aspects of it which deserve our formal attention. It would not seem accidental that the Risen Jesus' ministry to the Emmaus disciples has two parts, teaching and meal-sharing. One is tempted here to think of the shape of christian liturgy, which begins with hearing and studying the Word of God and which concludes with shared table fellowship, either the agape meal and/or the eucharist. Three points, then, deserve attention: a) the **teaching** of the Scriptures in 24:25-27, b) the **eucharistic** character of the meal in 24:30-31 and c) the repeated **link** in Luke-Acts **between word and meal.**

First, one of the striking things about Luke's version of the Easter events is the repeated emphasis placed on understanding "the word," either the word of the Scriptures or Jesus' own word:

Angel Reminds (24:6-7)	*Jesus Teaches* (24:25-27)	*Jesus Teaches* (24:44-47)
"Remember how he told you, while he was still in Galilee, that the Son of Man must be delivered into the hands of sinful men and be crucified, and on the third day rise." And they remembered his words.	"O slow of heart to believe all that prophets have spoken! Was it not necessary that the Christ suffer and enter into his glory?" And beginning with Moses and all the prophets, he interpreted in all the scriptures the things concerning himself.	"These are my words which I spoke to you, while I was still with you, that everything written about me in the law of Moses and the prophets and the psalms must be fulfilled." Then he opened their minds to understand the scriptures.

It is no exaggeration to say that the first task of Jesus in his conversation with these Emmaus travellers is to teach them the correct meaning of God's Scriptures. They had confessed Jesus as a "prophet mighty in word and deed" (24:19), whose death seemingly contradicted that confession. The theme of Jesus' word to them addressed just this misinterpretation of his death. In support of their belief that Jesus is indeed God's great prophet, the Risen Lord tells them to read the prophets correctly: "O foolish men, and slow of heart to believe all that the prophets have spoken!" (24:25). The death of Jesus does not disqualify him from being God's anointed one. On the contrary, it is proof that he really is the Christ: "Was it not necessary that the Christ should suffer these things and enter into his glory?" (24:26). And so Jesus proceeds to instruct these disciples in the correct reading of God's word, which will show that he is indeed God's prophet and Christ: "And beginning with Moses and all the prophets, he interpreted to them in all the scriptures the things concerning himself" (24:27). The first Easter sermon, then, was preached by Jesus hismelf, as he expounded the Scriptures.

Second, when one compares 24:30-31 with unmistakable references to the eucharist, such as 22:19, one easily notes a remarkable parallelism in the key verbs of the narrative.

The Last Supper (22:19)	*The Emmaus Meal (24:31)*
And he **took** bread	he **took** the bread
and when he had **given thanks**	and **blessed,**
and **gave** it to them	and **gave** it to them

This is not a meal, the consumption of which is intended to disprove the possibility that the Risen Jesus was merely a "ghost," as will be the case with the eating scene in 24:41-43. This account completes the ministry of Jesus to the Emmaus disciples, and so functions as the complement of the instruction on the Scriptures in 24:25-27. In this light, the symbolic character of the meal should be highlighted, hence the patent allusions to sacred food or eucharist.

Third, it is a common feature of Luke-Acts to show the followers of Jesus at unity both in doctrine and at table. The premier example, of course, is the narrative in Lk 22:14-38, in which Jesus gives the disciples not only eucharistic food (22:19-20) but also specific christian teaching (22:24-38). Reinforcing this, Acts relates that immediately after the Pentecost speech of Peter, the new group of Jesus' followers was one in teaching and table fellowship: "And they devoted themselves to the apostles' **teaching** and fellowship, and the **breaking of bread** and the prayers" (Acts 2:42).

In a comparable passage, Paul is described conducting a christian meeting at Troas. The date is important, "the first day of the week" (Acts 20:7), suggesting the christian day of worship, the Easter day. As Paul taught or preached about Jesus for quite a long time, "he prolonged his speech until midnight" (20:7b), which occasioned the young man Eutychus to doze and fall out of the window of the room where they were gathered. After reviving him, Paul continued to teach and also to share fellowship with the group: "And when Paul had gone up and had **broken bread** and **eaten**, he **conversed** with them a long while, until daybreak" (20:11). Jesus' action of teaching and meal sharing in Luke, then, would seem to be a paradigm for the action of the young church as illustrated by the stories about Peter and Paul in Acts.

Although it is not clear whether the "breaking of the bread" described in Acts always refers to the christian eucharist, we are on firmer ground with Jesus' meal with the Emmaus disciples in Lk 24:30-31. An important piece of evidence comes from a passage in Acts which is deliberately parallel to Lk 24:13-35, viz. Philip's dealings with the Ethiopian eunuch in Acts 8:26-40. Let us first note the striking parallels and then draw the interpretative conclusions.

Luke 24:13-35	*Acts 8:26-40*
1. scene: on the way from Jerusalem (24:13)	1. scene: on the way from Jerusalem (8:26)
2. two disciples pondering the death of Christ (24:14)	2. a man pondering the suffering and death of God's servant (8:27-28)
3. Jesus, disguised, draws near (24:15)	3. Philip draws near (8:29-30)
4. Jesus asks them: "What is this conversation which you are holding?" (24:17)	4. Philip asks the eunuch: "Do you understand what you are reading?" (8:30)

5. answer from the disciples (24:18-24)

5. response from the eunuch (8:31)

6. Jesus explains the Scripture from a Christological perspective: "Beginning with Moses and all the prophets, he interpreted to them in all the Scripture the things concerning himself" (24:25-27)

6. Philip explains Isaiah as a prophecy of Jesus: "Beginning from this Scripture he preached Jesus to him" (8:32-34)

7. Apology: the Messiah's suffering leads to glory (24:26)

7. Apology: suffering of the Christ explained (8:32-33)

8. Request by disciples that Jesus stay with them at the inn (24:28-29)

8. Request by the eunuch that Philip sit with him in his chariot (8:31)

9. Eucharist, which signals that the despairing disciples are reintegrated as genuine believers in Jesus (24:30-31)

9. Baptism, which signals that the eunuch is incorporated as a true believer in Jesus (8:36-38)

10. Eyes opened (24:31)

10. Understanding gained (8:35-36)

11. Jesus' sudden disappearance (24:35)

11. Philip's sudden disappearance (8:39-40)

These striking parallels suggest many things to the careful interpreter of the gospel narrative, but one of the chief things may be the focus by Luke on the rites described, either the rite whereby strangers are incorporated as followers of Jesus (baptism, Acts 8:36-38) or the rite whereby full communion of mind and heart is symbolized (eucharist, Luke 24:30-31). The point is, since parallels are intentionally and carefully drawn by the author of Luke-Acts, when we see an obvious reference to the christian rite of baptism in Acts 8:36-38, we are surely intended to recognize a comparable rite in the narrative in Luke 24:30-31. If the remarks about baptism are patent in 8:36ff, there is warrant then for a reading of 24:30-31 as eucharist.

If time allowed, we could investigate the close community bonding symbolized by common teaching and shared table. For it is well known that Jewish teaching (Torah) is often described as bread, so that Lady Wisdom invites learners to come to her table and feed. People of like mind tend to reflect that unity in shared meals together. In fact, the converse would be true as well, only those may eat together who share the same teaching. In either case, the disciples with whom Jesus eats at Emmaus are shown by the very act of eating with Jesus to be restored disciples, true believers in the Risen Lord and genuine members of his covenant community. Shared teaching and shared table fellowship are both ministerial actions of the Risen Jesus and symbols of complete membership in Jesus' following. The narrative about the Emmaus disciples, then, is cast in a literary form which describes 1) the mission of the church (preaching the crucified Jesus) and 2) stages of the process of incorporating converts into the group (initiatory rites and eucharist). The "form," then, reflects actual church life and praxis.

Redaction

It is always hazardous to isolate a particular text-segment from its larger context, and never more so than with 24:13-35. We can gain considerable insight and appreciation of the Emmaus story if we try to see the typical patterns, phrases and themes of the whole gospel which are gathered there, like a bouquet of Luke's best flowers. For the specific details of this narrative bear the stamp of Luke's characteristic way of telling the general gospel story.

The Way ... on the Way. In his account of Jesus' ministry, Luke has a lengthy section which is not found in any of the other gospels, the "great interpolation" (9:51-18:14), the chief characteristic of which is the description of Jesus **on the way** to Jerusalem and Jesus' **way** or teaching on discipleship. Christians, of course, are called "The Way" in Acts (16:17; 18:25-26; 24:14, 22), a term which describes both their **way** of doing things (Jesus' teaching) and also their **way of mission and pilgrimage.** So it helps to recognize 24:13-35 as another story illustrating Jesus **on the way** and teaching **the way.**

Jesus' actions in the Emmaus story are actions of ministry, even the typical ministry that he exercised in his Galilee career. In particular, Jesus' pursuit of the wayward disciples strikingly resembles Jesus' earlier parable in 15:3-7 of the shepherd who went in search of lost sheep until he found them and returned them to the fold. Jesus, of course, ate with tax collectors and sinners (5:30; 7:34; 15:2; 19:7), which surely should include the Emmaus disciples, for they had lost faith and given up membership in Jesus' group—serious sins indeed. Yet Jesus preaches to them and shares table fellowship with them. The ministry to sinners and to the lost, then, continues even on Easter.

In the conversation with the unrecognized Lord, Clopas speaks about Jesus, but in a way which is quite ironic. He has apparently lost faith in Jesus because of his crucifixion, and so he is symbolically going away from Jesus and his followers. Yet what Clopas says about Jesus, while "old" news about his ministry, is nevertheless still true. He may not be a full believer in Jesus now, but ironically Clopas tells the gospel truth about him. Let us look at his account of Jesus more closely as a Lukan compendium of key gospel statements about Jesus.

A Prophet. Throughout this gospel, Luke has acclaimed Jesus as a prophet. Like Elisha and Elijah (4:21-27), the scope of his prophetic mission includes non-Jews as well as God's covenant people. And like the prophets of old, he performs many miracles, such as the cleansing of a leper or the raising of a dead son (7:16; 17:11-19); like a prophet, he proclaims God's law and calls down woe on sinners (10:13-15; 19:41-44). And like the prophets of old, he is a *rejected* prophet, who suffers innocently at the hands of sinful Jerusalem (13:33-35; Acts 7:52). And so, when Jesus is acclaimed "a prophet, mighty in word and deed," the reader of Luke's gospel realizes how appropriate such a title truly is for Jesus.

Mighty in Word and Deed. At the very beginning of his career (4:18-19), Jesus proclaimed in the synagogue a text of Isaiah which programmatically described his future mission. According to the prophecy, Jesus was commissioned to be mighty in word and deed: (a) *word*: "to preach the good news to the poor ... to proclaim the acceptable year of the Lord" and (b) *deed*: "recovering of sight to the blind ... liberty to those who are oppressed." This double theme of "mighty in word and deed" is captured again in the summary of Jesus' prophetic actions which is sent back to John the Baptizer in 7:22-23. (a) *Deeds*: "the blind receive their sight, the lame walk, lepers are cleansed, the deaf hear and the dead are raised up"; (b) *word*: "and the poor have the good news preached to them." What Clopas says of Jesus the prophet, then, is quite correct, even if he no longer believes it.

Set Israel Free. At the beginning of the gospel, Jesus is acclaimed by God's angels as "a Savior, Christ the Lord" (2:11). He is the object of attention from God's prophets, Simeon and Anna, who have made a lifetime of "looking for the consolation of Israel" (2:25) and "the redemption of Jerusalem" (2:38). Jesus indeed acts as Savior in his ministry of healing and forgiving, but especially on the cross when he proclaims to the thief that he will be with Jesus in paradise today (23:43). And Luke the evangelist proclaims Jesus as the unique and necessary savior of all in Acts 4:11-12 and 13:38-39. He truly does "set Israel free," perhaps not from the occupying army of the Romans, but free from sin, disease and death.

Clopas, therefore, functions as a type of evangelist of major Lukan statements about Jesus, an ironic evangelist who no longer believes in the one of whom he speaks so glowingly. Clopas spoke of Jesus' ministry of powerful deeds and persuasive preaching (24:19), which corresponds to the first half of the gospel, that is, to Jesus' Galilean ministry. But he also tells of Jesus' rejection, death and even his resurrection (24:20-24), which corresponds to the second half of the gospel, Jesus' career in Jerusalem. If Clopas repeats the gospel about Jesus' ministry in Galilee, Luke portrays Jesus himself as the spokesman who tells Clopas and all the gospel readers the full meaning of the Jerusalem events in Jesus' career. So, now we examine Jesus' own "christology," just as we did Clopas'.

Christ Must Suffer. The substance of Jesus' Easter message lies in the important demand that his rejection and death should be seen as part of God's providential plan. When the text says "the Christ **must** suffer," this is a typical way in which Jews referred to God as the agent of this action; for, since it was forbidden to use the sacred name of God, circumlocutions were found, such as **must** or the use of the passive voice "Abraham **was justified**" (by God). The evangelist prepared the reader to understand this type of expression by insisting earlier in the narrative that Jesus' death belongs to God's plan. Jesus himself actually predicts his passion, indicating its place in God's providence: "The Son of Man **must** suffer many things ... " (9:22; see 9:44 and 18:31-34). This is no minor theme for Luke, as it becomes one of the elements of the preaching of the apostles in Acts. On Pentecost, Peter tells the crowds, "this Jesus, delivered up according to the definite plan and foreknowledge of God" (2:23), insisting that the cross should *not* be a scandal or stumbling block to Israel (see Acts 4:28).

In God's plan, suffering has always been the fate of God's messengers and saints. Of God's prophets, Jesus remarks how Jerusalem has always "killed the prophets and stoned those sent to you" (13:33), which was true of them as well as of John the Baptizer and even Jesus himself. Suffering, likewise, is the lot of God's saints. For example, Paul tells the church at Lystra and Iconium that "through many tribulations we **must** enter the kingdom of God" (Acts 14:22-23). What we learn from 24:25-26, then, are several important items. What the Risen Jesus tells these two disciples is no more than what the earthly Jesus repeatedly told his disciples (see 9:22). Jesus' suffering, moreover, neither cancels his claim to be God's Christ, nor does it cancel the claim of Jesus' followers to share in God's favor and blessings. Without fully explaining how all this works, Luke nevertheless insists that we give full attention to "the way" of God, to God's plan and providence in history, which includes suffering, even for God's Christ.

Moses and the Prophets. One of the great themes in Luke is the argument for Jesus' legitimacy as the one who fulfills the prophecies of the Scriptures. As we noted above, in his inaugural action in the synagogue of Nazareth, after Jesus read from the prophet Isaiah, he proclaims, "Today, this scripture has been fulfilled in your hearing" (4:21). And at the other significant rhetorical place, the end of the gospel, Jesus again instructs the disciples about God's Messiah from the Scriptures (24:44-47). The preaching of the first disciples in Acts about Jesus is always an argument that he fulfills the Scriptures (Acts 2:22-36; 3:18-26; 8:30-35; 13:16-41). In particular, Luke shows that the sufferings of God's Messiah are no argument against his legitimacy, but precisely his confirmation as Christ, for the essence of the Scriptures shows that the Christ must suffer and so enter into his glory.

Christology

Luke's account of Jesus' activity on the first Easter contains a compendium of most of the important things this evangelist would preach about Jesus. Let us, then, examine Lk 24:13-35 for the christology which it contains. For example, Jesus' ministry as shepherd to lost sinners in 24:13-35 is an important reminder by Luke that the Risen Jesus continues his ministry and has not abandoned the church. This is an important, consoling statement about Jesus, for later christians such as Luke and his audience might wonder if the golden age when Jesus was accessible and near is really over. No, it is not! For the Risen Lord continues the same ministry in the contemporary church which he exercised long ago in Galilee. He is still the shepherd who searches out the lost sheep.

Luke, moreover, summarizes the vital confession about Jesus in this story: how Jesus is God's prophet, mighty in word and deed, the savior of his people. He is still the one who eats with sinners and opens the eyes of the blind. He continues to be the true teacher of God's scriptural Word even as he is the model of God's plan that the Christ and all saints enter glory through suffering. The Risen Jesus, then, remains the Savior, the Shepherd, the Prophet. In short, most of the significant statements Luke would make about Jesus in the gospel are summarized in 24:13-35.

Ecclesiology

The Emmaus story tells us a great deal about the covenant community of Jesus' followers for whom Luke wrote. They are a church of sinners in need of preaching and conversion. They have a special and distinctive way of reading God's word in the Scriptures, which plausibly accounts for Jesus' shameful death on the cross. They are a group with definite rites, especially baptism and eucharist, which symbolize and effect the full integration of believers into the covenant of God. And they know that being a disciple of Jesus means glad membership in his covenant group, for the completion of the salvation of the Emmaus disciples is symbolized by their return to the assembled disciples in Jerusalem and their sharing of the good news about Jesus (24:33-35).

4

Luke 24:36-49
"The Risen Lord and His Church"

Luke likes to do things in two's: two annunciation stories, two birth narratives, two trials of Jesus, now two appearances of the Risen Jesus. The second appearance of Jesus in Luke 24:36-49 is both similar to the account in 24:13-35 and quite different—similar because the Risen Lord continues to teach his disciples the correct meaning of the Word of God, but different because in the latter manifestation, the Risen Lord formally commissions his disciples to preach, thus giving shape and structure to his church.

Structure

The account of Jesus' appearance to the assembled disciples in 24:36-49 has three parts, each of which has a different function:

  1) Jesus, a ghost? (24:36-43)
  2) Jesus, the teacher (24:44-46)
  3) Jesus, the Lord (24:47-49)

In the first scene, Luke slaps down the insinuation that maybe the early disciples did not see the risen Jesus but only his ghost. The chief argument against this comes in the proof offered by Jesus' eating. The ancient cosmos was divided into two worlds, the world of the living, where people ate, and the land of the dead, where food is not taken. To prove that he belongs back in the world of the living, not the dead, Jesus does what living people do, he eats (24:37-43). This interpretation of eating as proof of being alive stands behind the account of Jesus' raising to life of Jairus' daughter. Although the girl was clearly dead, Jesus raised her up; and as proof to all that she was back in the land of the living, Jesus commands that she be treated appropriately, and so he directs that she be given something to eat (see Mk 5:43). The first part of this story, then, serves an apologetic function to disprove that Jesus is a ghost and to prove that he is in the land of the living.

In the second part (24:44-47), Jesus acts as the great teacher of Israel that he always was. He teaches the correct reading of the Scriptures to his disciples, just as he did to the Emmaus pair in 24:25-27. The perspective here is much broader than that earlier instruction in 24:25-27, for the issue is not just the suffering of the Messiah, but *"everything* written about me in the law of Moses and the prophets and the psalms" (24:44). This is clearly intended as a summary of christian interpretation of the Scriptures, instances of which are found in the way the Hebrew Scriptures are interpreted in Acts. The function of 24:44-47, then, has an apologetic flavor, for surely the Scriptures are needed to deal with the shame of the cross and other difficult aspects of Jesus' life. But besides apology, there seems to be a strong teaching function to 24:44-47, for this material becomes the substance of the preaching of the followers of Jesus. Two functions, then, are found here, apologetic and kerygmatic.

The third part of the story (24:47-49) is more familiar to us, for in it Jesus commissions the apostles to a formal ministry. "You are witnesses of these things!" The confirmation of them as witnesses will occur when the promised Holy Spirit is finally poured on them, so that they become legitimated both by Jesus' commission and by the Spirit. An ecclesiological function, then, characterizes the third part of the story.

Form

Yet the whole narrative of 24:36-49 has a distinctive form to it, a form noted earlier apropos of Mt 28:16-20, the form of vocation commissioning. As we approach Luke's story, it is good to note that at the very beginning of this gospel, the evangelist has cast the narrative of Jesus' vocation in the very same form, so that both beginning and end of the gospel correspond formally, first Jesus' vocation and call and then that of his disciples.

Form	Luke 1:26-38	Luke 24:36-53
1. *Introduction*	1:26-27	24:33-36a
2. *Confrontation*	1:28	24:36b
Reaction	1:29	24:37
Reassurance	1:30	24:38-40
3. *Commission*	1:31-33	24:47-49
4. *Objections*	1:34	—————
Reassurance	1:35	24:49
Sign	1:36	—————
5. *Conclusion*	1:38	24:50-53

Knowledge of this form helps us to make sense of certain aspects of the narrative. For example, the reaction of the disciples ("unbelief for joy," 24:41) becomes less obscure when we recognize it as a typical confused *reaction* to the presence of something supernatural or heavenly suddenly appearing in our world. The double action of Jesus in 24:38-40, both the showing of his hands and feet and the eating of food, functions to *reassure* the disciples. The form indicates, moreover, that the *commissioning* of the disciples in 24:47-49 stands as the thematic focus of the story.

Commissioning, then, remains the chief function of the appearance of the Risen Jesus. Although it is briefly treated in 24:47-49, those verses have a major impact on the rest of Luke's story, the preaching in Acts of the Apostles by those commissioned in the gospel. Everybody knows that what constitutes a reliable, valid witness is eyewitness experience of the event or deed. Second hand reports or hearsay are simply inadequate for determining issues of fact (see the criteria for Judas' replacement in Acts 1:21-22). The events of 24:36-49 all contribute to the establishment of the apostles as valid witnesses with firsthand experience of the Risen Jesus. They **know** Jesus is not ghost, for they saw him eat. They truly **know** his teaching for they were the recipients of his special instruction on God's word; and they are officially recognized as ascribed leaders, made so by the Lord himself.

These points are made much of in Acts. For example, Luke calls attention to the many resurrection appearances of Jesus to the disciples in which he "presented himself alive after his passion *by many proofs*" (Acts 1:3). The word "proof" there is a technical term for incontrovertible, legal evidence which every court should accept. In Lk 24:37-43, the "proof" that Jesus is alive comes especially in the remark about his eating, a point to which Luke alludes later in Acts. In his speech to the centurion Cornelius, Peter again refers to the reliability of the apostolic witness which is based on commonly accepted proof. Peter knows unmistakably that God raised Jesus from the dead (10:40), for God manifested the Risen Lord "to us who were chosen by God as witnesses, who ate and drank with him after he rose from the dead" (10:41). *Proof* stands behind the word of the apostles.

The specific authorization of certain people as official witnesses is also a major theme in Acts. Besides the formal replacement of Judas by Matthias (Acts 1:20-26), Luke again and again calls attention to the formal commissioning of apostolic preachers. Acts opens with a repetition of Jesus' Easter commission to the apostles: "You shall be my witnesses in Jerusalem and in all Judea and Samaria and to the end of the earth" (1:8). The complete commission there corresponds fully to that in Lk 24:47-49.

Luke 24:47-49	*Acts 1:7-8*
1. repentance and forgiveness should be preached in his	1. . . .**in Jerusalem and in all Judea and Samaria and to**

name **to all nations, beginning from Jerusalem.**	**the ends of the earth**
2. You are witnesses of these things.	**2. You will be my witnesses**
3. I send the **promise** of my Father upon you; but stay in the city, until you are clothed with **power** from on high.	3. You shall receive **power when the Holy Spirit** has come upon you.

The apostles in Luke's gospel, then, are commissioned by Jesus and confirmed by God's Spirit for a universal mission, which is the basic theme of Acts of the Apostles.

Redaction

The final shape of the narrative in 24:36-49 was the responsibility of the evangelist Luke, and it is not surprising that many of the important themes and ideas of his two-volume work would be gathered at this climactic point and highlighted there. It is most helpful, then, to note these themes and ideas, for they are the spice of Luke's soup, the colors woven into patterns in his tapestry.

These Are My Words. The Risen Jesus plays a grand role on this "first day of the week" as a teacher. We saw earlier how Jesus instructed the Emmaus disciples about the Scriptures (24:25-27), a task which he continues with the assembly of apostles and disciples (24:44-46). But something else is added here, for the Risen Jesus insists that he is only reminding the disciples of what he has been telling them all along, "These are my words which I spoke to you while I was still with you" (24:44). This remark is all the more striking when we recall the words of the angels at Jesus' tomb who reminded the women of the same thing, "Remember how he told you, while he was still in Galilee . . . " (24:6). Two points are being made: first, the premier task of the angels and Jesus on Easter was the definitive teaching of Jesus' basic message which was the correct interpretation of the Scriptures as testimony about him; second, this teaching was seen as a "reminder" of what had been taught all along, and so continuity is seen between the career of the earthly Jesus and the ministry of the Risen Christ.

Everything Written Must Be Fulfilled. This refers to the interpretation of the scriptural prophecies which are now fulfilled in Jesus, a theme fundamental to Luke' story (1:68-74; 4:18-21). Why this theme? and what is its import? In the ancient world, novelty was basically suspect, for tradition reigned. The golden age lay in the past and the best we can hope to do in the present is to recover it or be faithful to it. Such a respect for tradition and things past indicates that all value and legitimacy tends to be found there. This effects Jesus and his message, for his value and legitimacy rest in his continuity with the past. And so the gospel begins with the note that Jesus is the legitimate heir of King David and the fulfillment of God's ancient promise to David about a successor to sit on his throne (1:32-33). In Jesus, Mary recognizes God's own "remembrance" of the great promises to Israel for a Savior (1:54; see 1:70, 73). And at his inaugural appearance in Nazareth's synagogue, Jesus claims legitimacy as the fulfillment of Isaiah's prophecy (4:18-21). The identity of Jesus, his role and his ministry, are all understood and valued precisely as they are seen as the fulfillment of God's Scriptures, for then God himself truly stands behind Jesus as the providence guiding him (see Acts 2:23), which gives us a powerful, apologetic explanation for his suffering and death. Jesus and Luke, then, appeal to the most widely accepted source of legitimacy, God's past Scriptures, to interpret, defend and promote Jesus.

He Opened Their Minds to Understand. Just as Jesus "opened the Scriptures" to the Emmaus disciples (24:32), so he opens the minds of his select disciples to understand his teaching and his identity. In one sense, this has been the major task of Jesus throughout his career, the preaching of God's word. Back in his inaugural preaching engagement, Jesus made it clear that God's Spirit was upon him for this very task, " ... to *proclaim* release to captives ...to *proclaim* the acceptable year of the Lord" (4:18-19). In another place Luke summarizes Jesus' ministry in terms of his preaching, "He went on through cities and villages, preaching and bringing the good news of the kingdom of God" (8:1). The Risen Jesus, then, continues to do for God's people what he always did, preach the good news and open human minds to understand.

The Christ Must Suffer. The early church was continually faced with the difficult task of making sense of Jesus' shameful death, "a stumbling block to Jews and folly to Greeks" (1 Cor 1:23). How could Jesus be God's holy one, Son and Prophet if he came to such a terrible end? And so one of the major tasks of early preachers was the apologetic treatment of his death, a task which might show three things. 1) His death is in accord with God's plan in the Scriptures, or 2) his death is patterned after the fate of Israel's great prophets, all of whom were rejected and killed, or 3) his death leads to glory. Philip catechizes the Ethiopian eunuch in Acts 8:30-33 about the suffering of the Isaian servant; Stephen notes that Israel rejected Moses (Acts 7:27, 35, 39) as well as all the other prophets (7:52), for it is the fate of authentic prophets to be dishonored, rejected and even killed by Israel (Lk 6:23; 13:34). In regard to 24:45, all through the gospel and Acts, Luke has mounted a consistent argument that God's Christ *must* suffer; in fact suffering is proof of his authenticity. So the Risen Jesus, when he teaches that God's Christ must suffer, knows whereof he speaks; his suffering is his "entrance into glory" (24:26), a process which applies to his followers as well as himself (Acts 14:22).

Repentance and Forgiveness of Sins Preached in His Name. It was the common point of view that humanity stood in need of reform and repentance. For example, the main theme of the preaching of John the Baptizer, a great popular revivalist of Jesus' time, was a baptism "of repentance for the forgiveness of sins" (3:3). This likewise became a major theme in the preaching of Jesus (see 13:3, 5; 15:7, 10). And mandated by the Risen Lord, it became a central theme of the apostles' preaching (24:47), who proclaimed that forgiveness can be found only in Jesus and nowhere else. When Peter's Pentecost speech about Jesus succeeds and the crowds ask what is the appropriate response to the gospel which they have heard, Peter replies, "Repent, and be baptized every one of you in the name of Jesus Christ for the forgiveness of your sins" (Acts 2:38). Peter's response, precisely because of its place in the first formal mission speech of the new church, has programmatic value as a summary of right thinking and right acting in response to the gospel.

Both Peter and Paul go on to argue with the synagogue Jews that forgiveness of sins is **uniquely** and **necessarily** found only in Jesus. For example, in Acts 4:11-12, Peter describes Jesus as the fulfillment of Ps 118:22, "The stone (Jesus) rejected (i.e. crucified) by the builders (the chief priests)." He goes on to explain more of the psalm which describes this stone as the "head of the corner," by which he means, "There is salvation in no other name under heaven given among humankind by which we must be saved" (4:12). **Jesus is the *unique* Savior.** Balancing this, Paul tells the synagogue at Antioch that "through this man forgiveness of sins is proclaimed among you, and by him every one that believes is freed from everything from which you could *not* be freed by the law of Moses" (13:38-39). **Jesus is the *necessary* Savior.** Just as Jesus commanded, the apostles indeed will preach repentance and forgiveness of sins which, as Acts shows, are uniquely and necessarily found only in Jesus.

To All Nations. The Risen Jesus commands a universal mission, just as the tradition in Mt 28:19 records. Although in Matthew there was evidence of an earlier tradition regarding a mission restricted to Jews only, Luke's version of the gospel indicates from its very beginning a universal scope to Jesus' mission, which then becomes the basis for the apostles' mission. The prophet Simeon prophesied about Jesus that he was to be "a light for revelation to the Gentiles and for glory to thy people Israel" (2:32), indicating at the very beginning of Jesus' career the breadth and scope of his mission. Simeon's prophecy is buttressed by Jesus' own later reference to other prophecies from the Scriptures about the prophets Elijah and Elisha who were sent to non-Jews (4:25-27), indicating an ancient pattern of universal mission. What applies to Jesus applies also to his disciples; they are commissioned by the Risen Jesus in Lk 24:47 and Acts 1:8 for a mission from Jerusalem to the ends of the earth, a mission which is obediently fulfilled first in the conversion of Cornelius by Peter in Acts 10 and later in the missionary journeys of Paul in Asia Minor, Greece, Malta and Italy.

I send the Promise of My Father. Jesus promises to send the Holy Spirit upon his disciples, to "clothe them with power from on high" for their mission. Several points need to be made here. First, it is the Risen Jesus who sends the Spirit. Peter makes this clear in his first speech in Acts, when he explains the Pentecost phenomenon to the crowds and preaches about Jesus: ". . . having received from the Father the promise of the Holy Spirit, he has poured out this which you see and hear" (2:33). This means that one of the main tasks of the Risen Jesus is to strengthen, guide and support his covenant community by the continual out-pouring of the Holy Spirit, an on-going ministry to God's people. Every mention of Spirit in Acts, then, should be seen as another instance of Jesus' continual ministry to his followers; for according to Luke, Jesus is the giver of Spirit to the church.

Second, we might ask what the purpose or function of Spirit is for Jesus' disciples? In part this has been answered already, for "spirit" means valid, *achieved* leadership status for the Lord's apostles, completing their *ascribed* status mandated by the same Jesus. They enjoy both criteria for leadership, and so are confirmed in their important roles. The gift of the Spirit also indicates that like Jesus, the apostles will function as prophetic "men of God," people endowed with power which makes them "mighty in word and deed." And so they will act boldly and powerfully, which actions will serve as their credentials to their listeners (see Lk 24:19; Acts 2:22). Spirit, moreover, will indicate that they are not sinners, but holy people who are set apart for sacred work. The crowds may consider them to be as ignorant fellows (Acts 4:13), disobedient people (Acts 5:28), and even sinful men, but that judgment does not square with God's assessment of them. On the contrary, God's spirit has been poured on them, indicating that they are "in the know," obedient to a heavenly power, and consecrated for holy tasks.

Christology

Because of the richness of the perspective in Lk 24:36-49, it is useful for us to ask about the composite picture of the Risen Jesus encoded in this narrative. Luke makes a series of remarkable statements about the Risen Jesus which will become the substance of Peter's and Paul's preaching in Acts. First, Luke proclaims that the Risen Jesus is present and active in the life of the church. There is no golden age in the past when Christians heard, saw and touched Jesus; the same Lord is present to his followers now and performs the same saving actions on their behalf today. In particular, Jesus teaches the true, if hidden meaning of God's Word, viz., how Moses, the Prophets and the Writings all prophesy about him. Jesus, moreover, is the Savior first heralded by God's angels (2:11) and now functioning as such to the apostles and the rest of the world, offering forgiveness of sins in his name. Furthermore, he is Lord of all people, savior and benefactor of all, just as he is judge of all (see Acts 10:42; 17:31). Finally, the Risen Jesus acts as Lord of God's covenant community, not only teaching God's Word but commissioning other preachers to summon the peoples of the world to conversion and membership with those who believe in God's Christ. This portrait, then, is no mere repetition of the tradition, but a rich, sophisticated development of christology.

Ecclesiology

If 24:36-49 conveys so much information about the Risen Jesus, it also tells us much about the covenant group which believes in this Risen Lord. According to the mission which Jesus commissions, the church is to be an inclusive group, from "all nations." The call of Jesus is a call to repentance and forgiveness of sins, implying a mission to sinners, to the lost, to apostate disciples. They are, moreover, the flock which is still tended by Jesus, who establishes firm leadership to serve and guide the church and who sends the Spirit to empower and confirm its symbolic leaders. For the Spirit sent upon the leaders will be sent upon the church at large ("for you shall receive the Holy Spirit," Acts 2:38). It is a gifted covenant community, in possession of God's scriptural word and made holy by the presence of God's Spirit. And it is a dynamic group, commissioned for bold proclamation of the gospel ("You are witnesses of these things!").

5

John 20:1-2, 11-18
"Jesus and Mary Magdalene"

Introduction

Understanding the Easter narratives in the Fourth Gospel is an exciting task, but one which requires careful attention to detail. When readers who are familiar with the individual details of the Easter narratives in the synoptic gospels turn to the Fourth Gospel, they are curiously struck by the sense of completeness of the Johannine version of those traditions. Things which were just mentioned in passing in Matthew or Luke tend to be narrated in full in the Fourth Gospel. Details left vague in the synoptics are given dramatic precision in John. One senses that John's version is the fullest account of the Easter events, a veritable compendium of what was only sketched here and there by the other evangelists. And for this reason the resurrection stories in the Fourth Gospel deserve our close attention.

For example, the Fourth Gospel records a Johannine version of two basic stories which are found in the synoptic accounts. All of the gospels narrate how certain women go to Jesus' tomb to anoint his body, how they find the tomb empty, and how an angel proclaims to them the raising of Jesus from the dead (Mk 16:1-8; Mt 28:1-8; Lk 24:1-8). Common to Matthew and Luke is an account of Jesus' appearance to his inner circle of disciples, which includes their formal commissioning as his messengers (Mt 28:16-20; Lk 24:36-49). As regards the women at the tomb, the Fourth Gospel records that only Mary Magdalene, not the other women came to an empty tomb (20:1-2); and this lone Mary is not given a proclamation about Jesus' resurrection by the angel who addresses her (20:11-13). As regards Jesus' appearance to his disciples, the Fourth Gospel narrates that Jesus appeared to them (20:19-23), although the substance of that visit differs from the report in Matthew and Luke. John's version, while "traditional," stands apart from the synoptic accounts in terms of both specific details and general substance. We shall pay particular attention to these two basic episodes in the following investigation of John's account of the resurrection stories.

The Fourth Gospel, moreover, echoes in one document many of the individual details found here and there in the synoptic accounts. For example, both Matthew and John reflect what appears to be a rumor that Jesus' body was stolen from the tomb.

Matthew: Rumor of Theft	*John: Suspicion of Theft*
"Tell people, 'His disciples came by night and stole him away while we were asleep.'" So they took the money and did as they were directed; and this story has been spread among the Jews to this day (28:13-15; see also 27:62-66)	"They have taken the Lord out of the tomb, and we do not know where they have laid him" (20:2, 13, 15)

Both Luke and John record that, upon the report by the women, disciples ran to the tomb and found it empty, just as the women said:

Luke: Disciples at Tomb	*John: Two Disciples at Tomb*
Some of those who were with	So she ran, and went to

us went to the tomb, and found it just as the women had said, but him they did not see (24:24)

Simon Peter and the other disciple ... Peter then came out with the other disciple and they went toward the tomb (20:2-10)

Like Luke, John records that Jesus displayed his body to the disciples at his appearance to them, presumably as proof that he was not a ghost:

Luke: Jesus Shows His Body

John: Jesus Shows His Body

Jesus himself stood among them. But they were startled and frightened, and supposed that they saw a ghost. And he said to them, "Why are you troubled, and why do questionings rise in your hearts? See my hands and my feet, that it is I myself; handle me, and see; for a ghost has not flesh and bones as you see that I have"
(24:36-39).

Jesus came and stood among them and said to them, "Peace be with you." When he had said this, he showed them his hands and his side. Then the disciples were glad when they saw the Lord
(20:19-20).

And, like Luke, the Fourth Gospel records that Jesus appeared in Jerusalem, not Galilee, and on that same day, not a future time.

The point of this is not to argue that John might be more historically reliable than the synoptic evangelists, which may well be the case in some stories. But our investigation of the resurrection stories in the Fourth Gospel focuses precisely on the differences between John and the synoptics, not their points of contact. John's differences are clues and invitations to the careful reader to ask about the special way in which John tells these stories and to attend to the distinctive editorial touches which lie behind these differences.

Rather than blend the gospels together for what common message they might tell us, modern readers are careful to inquire about the distinctiveness of each evangelist, a point of view which proves to be immensely rewarding in the case of the Johannine version of the appearances of Jesus.

Structure

According to the Fourth Gospel, Jesus appears first to Mary Magdalene, a dramatic and touching narrative, but one which is fraught with problems and questions. Why is it only in the Fourth Gospel that the risen Jesus appears individually to Mary Magdalene? Does the fact that the recipient of the resurrection appearance is a woman have any bearing on how this story should be read? What are we to make of Jesus' announcement that he has "not yet ascended"? It is beyond this study to take up the historical questions raised by this story, but we are best advised to continue asking what this narrative would mean in a Johannine context for the specific group of believers who made up the community of the Fourth Gospel. To that end, let us continue asking of this story the kinds of critical, but enlightening questions we have asked of other documents.

The story of the appearance of the Risen Jesus to Mary Magdalene in the Fourth Gospel has four distinct parts:

(a) report by Mary to the disciples (20:1-2)
(b) angelic question (20:11-13)
(c) epiphany by Jesus to Mary (20:14-16)
(d) revelation of Jesus to Mary (20:17-18)

Report (20:1-2). Unlike the synoptic gospels, the Fourth Gospel states that Mary Magdalene alone, unaccompanied by other women, comes to the tomb on "the first day of the week." This might be a characteristic Johannine editorial technique of highlighting the importance of specific individuals, who become "typical' figures representing some character trait or theological position. Mary leaves the empty tomb and rushes to make a preliminary report to the disciples of Jesus, to "Simon Peter and the other disciple, the one whom Jesus loved" (v 2) about the apparent theft of Jesus' body.

Angelic Question (20:11-13). Unlike the synoptic accounts, Mary returns to the tomb. Peter and the Beloved Disciple have apparently come and departed (20:10) by the time Mary "stooped to look into the tomb." The traditional angels engage her, but their role differs in this narrative, for they do *not* proclaim Jesus' resurrection, but only engage her in a question-answer dialogue: "Why are you weeping?" "Because they have taken away my Lord . . . . "

Epiphany (20:14-16). A christological epiphany then takes place, as Jesus manifests himself to Mary, who appears to be, in her own right, a "beloved disciple" whom the Risen Jesus calls by name. Jesus' dialogue with Mary is remarkably parallel to the question-answer dialogue with the angels in the previous part of this narrative.

Angels & Mary (20:11-12)	*Jesus & Mary (20:15-16)*
1. *Question:*	1. *Question:*
"**Woman, why are you weeping?**"	"**Woman, why are you weeping?** Whom do you seek?"
2. *Answer:*	2. *Answer:*
"Because they have **taken away** my Lord, and I do not know **where** they **have laid him.**"	"Sir, if you have **carried** him **away,** tell me **where** you **have laid him,** and I will take him away."

Inasmuch as the answers to Mary's questions are given by Jesus alone, the Risen One remains in the Fourth Gospel the only revealer of important mysteries and truths. Disciples are bound immediately and personally to Jesus, the unique revealer of God (1:18).

Revelation (20:17-18). A remarkable revelation is given Mary, as well as a commission to proclaim that revelation. As happened in other resurrection stories, the risen Jesus commissions someone to speak about him: "Go to my brethren and say to them ... " (v 17a). And Mary is entrusted with a most remarkable message, one which in the Fourth Gospel transcends the mere report of Jesus' vindication and restoration: "Say to them, 'I am ascending to my Father and your Father, to my God and your God'" (v 17b).

In short, the structure of this story indicates a movement from panic and weeping to epiphany and revelation, from *not* knowing the place where Jesus is to knowing whither he is ascending, to the most important place in the cosmos. Mary, who initially had excusable, erroneous ideas about Jesus' status (theft of his body), eventually has extraordinary knowledge about Jesus' true position and status (ascension to God). She who reported only bad news and confusion returns to report one of the most important messages given anyone in the gospels. As the narrative stands, the adventures of Mary precede and follow the story about Peter and the Beloved Disciple; this type of sandwiching technique suggests that she is to be compared and contrasted with the two disciples. Unlike them, she is reported to have received a heavenly epiphany of the Risen Jesus and a solemn revelation; "'I have seen the Lord!' And she told them that he had said these things to her" (20:18), which suggests that she enjoys an extraordinary status in a gospel where correct and special knowledge about Jesus denotes one's standing in the group.

Source

Although it is not our intention to pursue questions of history, it is important for understanding the editorial intent of this account to compare and contrast it with the other accounts of what is said to have happened to the faithful women who came to Jesus' tomb. For in this way, we may sharpen our appreciation of the meaning and significance of the Johannine version in 20:1-2, 11-18 vis-à-vis its theological and social horizon of the Johannine community.

Mk 16:1-8 reports that three women, not just Mary Magdalene, went to the tomb, which was empty. There a single angelic figure solemnly proclaimed that Jesus was raised, after which the women were told to remind Peter and the other disciples that Jesus will rendezvous with them in Galilee. The women fled in fear and told no one. Mark, then, reports: 1) *no* appearance by Jesus to these women; 2) *no* commissioning to herald a specific message; 3) insistence that these women said nothing.

Mt 28:1-10 basically repeats Mark's version, emphasizing the role of the angel as the opener of the tomb and the proclaimer of Jesus' resurrection. The women in Matthew, who departed with "fear and great joy," are then met by Jesus himself. There is no question here of mistaken identity (see Lk 24:16; Jn 21:4), for the women immediately recognize him, take hold of his feet and worship him (28:9). Jesus speaks to them, but his message only repeats what the angel had told them, a pattern we noted above in John 20:11-12 and 15-16.

Angel to Women (28:5-7)	*Jesus to Women (28:10)*
Do not be afraid ...	**Do not be afraid;**
go quickly **and tell**	**go and tell**
his disciples that he	**my brethren**
has risen from the dead;	
and behold, he is going	
before you **to Galilee;**	**to go to Galilee**
there you will see him.	and **there they will see me.**

This type of comparison suggests that the angelic proclamation to the women was sufficient and so the reinforcement by Jesus lacks a certain specialness which is found in the Jesus-Mary dialogue in Jn 20:15-18. If some sort of commission is alluded to in Mt 28:9-10, it is certainly of a modest sort, unlike the importance given Mary in Jn 20. In short, Matthew reports that 1) Jesus *does* appear, 2) to *all* the women, not just Mary, and 3) the *message* Jesus gives is only a repetition of the angelic message, not a special revelation.

Lk 24:1-11 tells quite a different story. The women's identity is insignificant; they are not named at the beginning of the story (v 1), but identified later almost as an after-thought (v 10). The role and importance of the angel is enhanced in Luke's version, for the angel not only gives the traditional proclamation about Jesus' resurrection and im-minent appearance in Galilee, but functions as a "reminder" of Jesus' words: "Remember how he told you, while he was still in Galilee, that the Son of Man must be delivered into the hands of sinful men, and be crucified, and on the third day rise" (24:7). This angel, then, actually catechizes the women, and on the strength of their new faith, they become believers, "And they remembered his words, and returning ... they told all this to the eleven and to all the rest" (24:8-9). In this aspect, the angel is similar to Jesus, who said the same thing to the disciples at his appearance late that same Easter evening; this message, moreover, is no new revelation, only a conscious "remembering" of what was often said in the past.

Angel to Women (24:6-7)	*Jesus to Disciples (24:44-46)*
Remember how **he told you, while he was still in Galilee,**	These are **my words which I spoke to you, while I was still with you . . .**
that the Son of man **must be delivered** into the hands of sinful men, and be crucified,	that the Christ **must suffer**
and **on the third day rise.**	and **on the third day rise** from the dead.

The message of the angel is identical with Jesus' own catechesis of his disciples: 1) remembering Jesus' words, 2) about the suffering of God's anointed one and 3) his resur-rection on the third day. Although the narrative clearly asserts that these women did not see Jesus himself, that point seems to be an important thematic factor in the story:

apparitions of the Risen Jesus are not common (see Acts 10:41), and perhaps not necessary. For what counts is that the disciples of Jesus speak about his death and resurrection, both from the Scriptures (24:25-27, 44-45) and from his own words (24:6-7, 44), and that hearers be moved to faith (see Acts 2). It is interesting to note that the report of the women is judged an "idle tale," not worthy of belief (24:11), a fate accorded the apostolic preaching in Acts as well. Luke, then, insists that 1) Jesus did *not* appear to the women, 2) who were reminded to *recover* Jesus' words, 3) which constitute *no new message*, but what the earthly Jesus had been saying all along.

The synoptic accounts, then, do not give a coherent report about the women at the tomb; in particular they are not in agreement on whether the women saw the risen Jesus or not; nor is it clear whether they were given a distinctive revelation to report or only a message for the disciples to gather in Galilee; nor is it clear whether they are peceived as being deputized to have an official role as heralds or only to serve as figures who advance the narrative by drawing others into the story.

In light of this synopsis, John 20:1-2, 11-18 has many distinctive aspects which probably indicate the specific theological and social character of that gospel. 1. Only Mary Magdalene —not three women— is featured. 2. Jesus both reveals himself to her and reveals to her a remarkable message, thus reducing the role of the angel at the tomb to insignificance. 3. She appears to have been given a distinctive role to play, the herald of a remarkable piece of information about Jesus. She is not the conveyor of an "idle tale," nor the deliverer of travel instructions to the disciples, but the reporter of a significant revelation from Jesus. To the trained eye, it would appear that the author of the Fourth Gospel was aware of the other traditions, but retold them in a distinctive way to convey the special interests and needs of the Johannine community. The distinctiveness of this traditional account in the Fourth Gospel invites us to search out its especial meaning by tracing what appear to be characteristic themes in the Fourth Gospel.

Redaction

If 20:1-2, 11-18 is looked at in terms of motifs and themes characteristic of the Fourth Gospel, the narrative's focus and importance can be more readily recovered. Let us survey several of the more important Johannine motifs.

I do not know. When Mary twice admits "I do not know" (20:2, 13), she echoes a major theme in the Fourth Gospel. It is no sin initially *not* to know whence Jesus comes and whither he goes, for disciples can be catechized and brought to light, as is the case with the Samaritan woman (4:7-26) and Thomas (14:5). Others in the gospel are hopelessly *not* in the know; Nicodemus, because he is flesh, cannot know what is spiritual or heavenly (3:6, 12). And so Jesus can reproach him, "Are you a teacher of Israel and you *do not know* this?" (3:10). And people who think according to fleshly standards also cannot know whence Jesus is, whither he goes or where he truly is (see 7:26-28; 6:41-42). Mary Magdalene, then, moves from admitting twice that "I do not know" to a position where she knows special information about Jesus, especially "whither" he has gone, "Say to them, 'I am ascending ... '" (20:17). She is uniquely "in the know."

A Typical Character. Commentators on the Fourth Gospel remind us that the *dramatis personae* of this gospel are representative figures who symbolize specific attitudes or themes. Nathanael, for example, represents a person who is not dissuaded by objections to the church's preaching about Jesus, but "comes and sees" for himself, for which Jesus praises him as "a true Israelite" (1:45-50). Mary Magdalene should be seen as an another typical or symbolic character in the Fourth Gospel, just like Thomas, Peter and the Beloved Disciple. She is decidedly an "insider," even a beloved disciple of Jesus. She "weeps" for Jesus (20:11), and he calls her by name, as a good shepherd calls his own sheep by name (see 10:3 and 20:16). She is, moreover, a "charismatic" individual, for she receives a personal epiphany immediately from the risen Jesus and a distinctive revelation to communicate to his disciples. Whereas Jesus made cryptic remarks about his death as glorification or lifting up, there is no hidden meaning whatever in the words of Jesus to Mary, "I am ascending ... " Jesus earlier predicted a glorious future time "when I shall no longer speak to you in riddles, but tell you plainly of the Father" (16:25). Jesus' unambiguous remarks to Mary suggest that she belongs in that special future time. The Fourth Gospel, then, portrays Mary as an enlightened individual who does not depend on the group or anyone else for her most sophisticated knowledge about Jesus; she receives immediately from the Risen Jesus both epiphany, revelation and commission— a charismatic figure of the highest order. In this she stands apart from and above the process praised in 20:29 (see 1:35-50), which will be described shortly, whereby ordinary folk do not see Jesus directly, but must depend on the mediation of him to them by church leaders and preachers.

Revelations. From other investigations, Mary is typical of the small number of strong individuals in the Johannine community, with the emphasis placed on "individual," personal or immediate links with Jesus, not communal allegiance with a group gathered in his name. After all, the branches of the vine draw life from adhering individually to Jesus, the vine, not to other branches (see 15:4-7). Regarding her distinctive character in the Fourth Gospel, it would seem that Jesus' epiphany and revelation to Mary carry much weight in this gospel. It is not so much a question of her being commissioned to a formal role in the group as was Peter (21:15-17), but an affirmation of where special status might lie in the Johannine community. Status, not offical role, seems at times to be based on achievement, not ascription. Mary's importance does not depend on an appointment by the earthly Jesus (see Mk 3:13-19; Mt 10:1-4), but is undergird by her charismatic experience of the Risen Lord. If, as seems to be the case in the Fourth Gospel, what is material, fleshly and earthly is **of no avail** (6:63; see 8:23), then importance and value are put on what is "spiritual." The epiphany of Jesus to Mary and the special revelation she received would classify her in the Johannine group as a "spiritual" person, out of the ordinary, even as a counter-cultural figure.

To a Woman. This gospel notes that Jesus gave special revelations to three women. The function of these revelations varied in each case, but always served to indicate the special status of these women as "insiders" in the Johannine group and even intimates with Jesus. For example, Jesus reveals to the Samaritan woman, who begins the story as an outsider (4:9), the fact that he is the Messiah (4:26), which revelation she immediately proclaims to others (4:29) and calls them to Jesus (4:39). To Martha, who was herself a "beloved disciple" (11:5), Jesus revealed that he is "the Resurrection and the Life" (11:25); Martha then went and called Mary to come to Jesus, a symbolic missionary action comparable to what the Samaritan woman did. Finally Mary Magdalene receives a revelation from Jesus about his "ascension," after which she is formally commissioned to proclaim this revelation to Jesus' disciples. The Samaritan Woman and Martha indeed went and "called" others to come to Jesus, but according to the text they were un-official, un-commissioned heralds. Mary Magdalene, how-ever, is offical in some sense, as Jesus formally commands her "Go to my brethren and say to them ... " (20:17).

	Christological Revelation	*Commission Role or Office*
Samaritan Woman	Messiah	unofficial missionary
Martha	I am the Resurrection and the Life	unoffical missionary
Mary Magdalene	I am ascending	official prophet

The gospel, then, contains three instances of Jesus giving a personal revelation to women, who function as proclaimers of that revelation and who act as missionaries to lead others to Jesus. Even if these revelations do not formally commission the Samaritan Woman and Martha with an official role in the church, they do sugggest the high status these women enjoyed. By virtue of Jesus' command, however, Mary Magdalene's status is official even if her precise role is unusual and controversial. Yet as we compare this pattern in John with the synoptic gospels, we immediately note how exceptional it is; and so we take note of how untypical such stories are—they were not the norm. This type of investigation, therefore, suggests that this Johannine community was unusual in terms of its social organization, for which this document has earned the soubriquet of "the Maverick Gospel."

Christology

Since much is made in this discussion of the special revelation of the risen Jesus to Mary Magdalene, it would seem worth our while to examine the content of his remarks. Jesus told her: "I am ascending to my God and your God, to my Father and your Father" (20:17). Although the word "ascend" appears here, it is not the technical term which is found elsewhere in the New Testament for Jesus' being taken up to heaven by God (see Mk 16:19; Acts 1:2, 11, 22; Eph 4:8-9; 1 Tim 3:16). In Jn 20:18, Jesus is not passively taken up to heaven (*analambano:* "to take up") but goes up on his own accord (*anabaino:* "to go up"). The first important clue, then, is the active quality of Jesus' ascent to God by his own power, a point which is important in the Fourth Gospel's christology.

This is not the first occurrence of this term "ascend" (*anabaino*) in the Fourth Gospel. In the earlier dialogue between Jesus and Nicodemus, a question is raised about Jesus, "a teacher from God" (3:2). In what sense is Jesus

"from God"? Jesus explains this in such as a way as to
signal precisely how he is a unique figure: "*No one* has
ascended into heaven but he who **descended** from heaven,
the Son of man" (3:13). This statement insists that Jesus is
originally a heavenly figure who descends from heaven and
then re-ascends, a point which makes him superior to all
patriarchs or prophets who are said to have gone up to
heaven for mystical revelations. So at the gospel's beginning,
Jesus is portrayed as the one who descends from heaven.
Yet, he will ascend when his mission is over. At the beginning of the Passion Narrative, it is noted that Jesus was
aware "that he had come from God and was going to God"
(13:3), so the reader expects his **ascension** to occur in the
context of his passion and death. In fact, when hostility and
rejection build, we are told that Jesus almost longs to
ascend back to his place with God, which is above earthly
hatred and conflict. To dropouts from his group who reject
his "Bread of Life," he says, "What if you were to see the
Son of man **ascending** to where he was before?" (6:62), a
statement which reaffirms that he was originally a heavenly
figure who descended to earth. Let us not forget that no
other gospel describes Jesus as an original heavenly figure
who **descends** and then **ascends** back to his original place.
After all, only the Fourth Gospel explicitly confesses Jesus
as "God" (1:1-2) and "Lord and God" (20:28).

But what was the place from which Jesus descended? Or
rather, what was the status Jesus had before he descended?
The Fourth Gospel begins with a statement that Jesus was
"in the bosom of the Father" (1:18), even face-to-face with
God (1:1-2). In other words, Jesus shared God's throne in
the center of heaven, a vision of which is promised to Jesus'
disciples in 1:51. This gospel, moreover, tells us that Jesus
prays for his return to that exalted position, even as he
enters his passion: "Father, glorify me in your own presence
with the glory which I had with you before the world was
made" (17:5). Jesus' status before he descended, then, was
one of glory beside God. And so, when Jesus tells Mary that
he is **ascending** to God, that assertion summarizes the

remarkable christology of the Fourth Gospel which acclaims Jesus as a heavenly figure, even "God" and "Lord and God" whose natural place is face-to-face with God. And the fact that Jesus ascends back to God on his own power further strengthens the appreciation of Jesus as a dynamic active agent of his own career. He has power to lay down his life and power to take it back (10:17-18); he has power to rise from the dead and to ascend back to his original place.

If this assessment of Jesus' message to Mary is correct, she is credited with knowledge about Jesus' heavenly status which is comparable to Thomas' confession in 20:28. She knows the most important things about Jesus in the Fourth Gospel, which indicates her special status as a receiver of heavenly revelations. A complete appreciation of the social import of this revelation to Mary Magdalene must wait until we deal with the symbolic importance and role of the Beloved Disciple. For we hope to show that, like the Beloved Disciple, Mary Magdalene is characterized in 20:1-2, 11-18 as a "spiritual" or charismatic person who is gifted with unique revelations by the risen Jesus of things that the early disciples either did not understand or did not know.

6

John 20:19-29
"Jesus, the Disciples, and Thomas"

In the Fourth Gospel, the narrative of Jesus' appearances to his disciples comes in two installments which are intended as complementary stories. First Jesus manifested himself to the disciples (20:19-23) with Thomas absent; eight days later, Jesus returns to the same disciples, but the scene ignores them and concentrates only on the dialogue between Thomas and Jesus (20:24-29). The first appearance ends with the disciples telling Thomas the gospel truth about the Risen Jesus ("We have seen the Lord," 20:25), which message he does to accept from the offical heralds; the second appearance ends with Jesus proclaiming "Blessed" those who do hear and accept the preaching about him without seeing him (20:29), thus stitching the two stories together in terms of both theme and the ordinary way people come to faith. We can, moreover, clarify the complementary character of the two narratives by investigating the literary form in which they are told.

Form

Like Mt 28:16-20, the two combined narratives of the manifestation of the Risen Jesus in John 20 clearly resemble the form of a vocation commissioning.

Form:	*John 20:19-29*
1. Introduction	20:19a
2. Confrontation	20:19b
Reaction	20:19c
Reassurance	20:20
3. Commission	20:21-23
4. Objection	20:24-25
Reassurance	20:26
Sign	20:27-29

Introduction. Jesus' appearance causes no little consternation among the disciples. This requires a word of *reassurance,* "Peace be with you!" which is followed by a gesture of *reassurance,* the showing of Jesus' hand and side, proof that the person appearing is truly Jesus and no one else, certainly not a ghost.

Commission. The focus of this resurrection manifestation rests characteristically on the *commissioning* of the disciples, "As the Father has sent me, so I send you," a commissioning confirmed by the gift of the Holy Spirit (20:22). Like the commissioning in Lk 24:36-49, three points are made: a) the apostles are formally commissioned (Jn 20:21//Lk 24:48, b) to preach repentance and forgiveness of sins (Jn 20:23//Lk 24:47), and c) they are confirmed by Jesus' sending of the Holy Spirit (Jn 20:22//Lk 24:49)

Objection. Yet *objections* are raised, not by the commissioned apostles, but by the absent Thomas, who doubts the reality of the Risen Lord, "Unless I see in his hands the print of the nails, and place my finger in the mark of the nails, and place my hand in his side, I will not believe" (20:25)

Reassurance. Characteristic of heavenly commissions, concession is made to such objections; and so Jesus returns to *reassure* Thomas (20:26-27).

Sign: And he offers Thomas a *sign* which should confirm his presence and his ability to commission his followers to proclaim him alive, "Put your finger here, and see my hands; and put out your hand, and place it in my side" (20:27). This gesture of reassurance has its desired effect, as Thomas fully accepts the presence of the Risen Jesus (20:28). The narrative in 20:19-29, then, employs a traditional and easily recognized form to convey the structure and import of the appearances of the Risen Jesus. The two appearances, moreover, are intended as complementary stories.

Redaction

Although the commissioning of the apostles is important in this gospel, it is not the only or premier focus in 20:19-29. Let us take another look at some of the major elements and themes in this narrative to see what special function these stories played in the Fourth Gospel. For the way the episodes are narrated here provides clues to a still richer story.

A Typical Character. As in the case of Mary Magdalene, Thomas functions in the Fourth Gospel as a typical, representative figure. According to the logic of John's narrative, Thomas has long been associated with Jesus' death but in an unknowing or ambivalent way. We first see Thomas on the occasion of Lazarus' illness and death, at first not understanding that Lazarus has truly died (11:12), and then glibly agreeing to follow Jesus on his return to hostile Judea, where ironically death awaits him, not Lazarus. Thomas' remark, "Let us also go, that we may die with him" (11:16), while bold in one sense, seems unenlightened and ambiguous. Later, in Jesus' Farewell Discourse to the apostles, the Master tells them that he is "going away" (i.e. death) and that they know the way (14:3). Thomas replies, "We do *not* know where you are going; how can we know the way?" (14:5), a very damaging statement in the Fourth Gospel, for it implies that Thomas is ignorant of the most basic data about Jesus, especially insight into his death and return to God. Thomas, then, is portrayed as a figure associated with Jesus' death, either *not* "in the know" and unenlightened about Jesus' death or unbelieving that Jesus has in fact conquered death (20:25). Yet the evangelist has carefully prepared the reader to associate Thomas with Jesus' death, either a glib remark about it or a radical misunderstanding of it. And so the singling out of Thomas in 20:24-29 for a special revelation about Jesus' triumph over death is most appropriate. He becomes the premier interpreter of Jesus' death in the Fourth Gospel.

The Others Told Him, 'We have seen the Lord'. Like so many things in this remarkable gospel, this innocent remark conveys important information, for it represents a basic pattern in the gospel about the typical way that the good news about Jesus was spread. The evangelist programmed the reader concerning this pattern back in the gospel's beginning, the inaugural events of Jesus' ministry in 1:35-51 where the narrative carefully establishes an important pattern: 1) believers speak about Jesus to others, 2) inviting them to come and see; 3) it may happen that certain hearers object to the gospel preached to them; 4) but they all finally come to Jesus and see for themselves, 5) who in turn confirms them with a word of commission or praise.

1. *Preaching by a believer*	1:35	1:41	1:43	1:45
2. *Invitation to come & see*	1:39	——	——	1:46
3. *Objections*	——	——	——	1:46a
4. *Coming to Jesus*	1:39b	1:42	——	1:47ff
5. *Confirmation*	1:39c	1:42b	1:43b	1:47b

This pattern is quite unusual when compared with the opening scenes in the synoptic gospels, for in them Jesus himself does the preaching and the calling; but in the Fourth Gospel things are otherwise. A pattern is established that faith comes from hearing the word preached by the church, a pattern which is not ignored in the rest of this gospel. The story of the Samaritan Woman verifies the pattern: having become a believer, she preaches about Jesus to those of her village, " . . . a man who told me all that I ever did. Can this be the Christ?" (4:29b). The villagers are invited to come and see for themselves, "Come, see a man . . . " (4:29a). The Samaritans indeed "believed in him because of the woman's testimony" (4:39) and "came to him" (4:40). They receive a confirmation of their belief in Jesus, for he stays two days with them and "many more believed because of his word" (4:42); in fact, their faith grows. "It is no longer because of your words that we believe, for we have heard for ourselves and we know that this is indeed the Savior of the World" (4:42).

The pattern which occurred in the beginning of the gospel returns at its conclusion—a major rhetorical clue to its importance. The pattern is supposed to apply to the narrative about Thomas and the other disciples in 20:24-29, but in a curious way. As believers with immediate experience of Jesus, the disciples to whom Jesus appeared in 20:19-23 preach the news of his resurrection to an unbeliever, Thomas: "We have seen the Lord" (20:25a). Ideally, Thomas should believe the apostolic preaching, and thereby deserve Jesus' blessing (20:29). But instead, Thomas offers objections, "Unless I see in his hands the print of the nails . . ." (20:25b). Inverting the pattern, Jesus comes to him (20:26-27) instead of Thomas coming to him, and Jesus leads him to faith, "My Lord and my God" (20:28). The story ends with solemn endorsement of the need to accept the word of others who preach about Jesus, "Blessed are those who have not seen and yet believe" (20:29), a word which confirms the process which has recurred again and again in the Fourth Gospel. The important factor here is to note how Thomas both confirms and breaks the pattern. On the one hand, Jesus' remark to Thomas in 20:29 confirms the basic pattern that faith comes from hearing the word preached about Jesus and the process whereby believers lead unbelievers to faith. But the direct revelation to Thomas upsets the pattern for it implies that some people are gifted with immediate experiences of Jesus and they learn directly from Jesus things not communicated by other ordinary disciples.

My Lord and My God. Yet we are not finished with this rich narrative, for as a result of Jesus' special christophany to Thomas, the newly believing disciple utters the most profound confession of Jesus' divinity. In the prologue, Jesus is the Word who is God (1:1-2), and at the end of the gospel, Jesus is "Lord" and "God" (20:28). But what is contained in Thomas' confession? In general, the God of Israel was said to exercise two basic powers in the world, *creative power* whereby God made the world and maintained it and *eschatological power* whereby God judged the world at the end of time. Each of these powers had a special name in Jewish theology; the deity was called "God" in virtue of *creative power* and "Lord" or executive in virtue of *eschatological power*.

The Fourth Gospel argues in 5:19-29 that Jesus is truly "equal to God," equal because he has creative power (5:19-20) and because he has eschatological power (5:21-29). And so, when in the gospel's prologue Jesus the Word creates the world (1:1-3) he is rightly called "God." It takes much time for the gospel to finally demonstrate that Jesus has *all* of the aspects of eschatolgoical power: 1) power to call the dead from their tombs (5:25//11:43-44), 2) power to judge (5:22 & 27//8:26ff), 3) power to have life in himself (5:26//10:17-18), and 4) the right to honor equal to God's (5:23). The true test of Jesus' eschatological power is his own death; but this gospel maintains that Jesus indeed has total power over death, power to lay down his life and power to take it back again (10:17-18). And so, when he appears to Thomas, the final demonstration has taken place: Jesus indeed has God's *eschatological power* to the full and so he should rightly be called by the traditional name of that power, "Lord." Thomas, then, becomes the proclaimer of the ultimate confession about Jesus: he is "God" because he has *creative power* and he is most assuredly "Lord" after his stunning demonstration of *eschatological power* in raising himself from the dead.

Christology

John 20:19-29 conveys many complex pieces of information about Jesus. Like other traditional narratives of Jesus' resurrection appearances, the Fourth Gospel portrays the Risen Jesus commissioning his disciples to preach. Like them, Jesus is the giver of God's Spirit, both to confirm the commissioned disciples and to indicate that their mission is one of "holiness," either the preaching of repentance for the forgiveness of sin (Lk 24:47), or the authority to deal with sin: "If you forgive the sins of any, they are forgiven; if you retain the sins of any, they are retained" (Jn 20:23). Yet these traditional features are quite surpassed in the Fourth Gospel when the narrative uses this traditional scene as the stage on which a christological confession is made which is not found in any of the other resurrection stories, viz., that Jesus is "Lord and God." In this confession, moreover, the Fourth Gospel differs from the synoptic traditions for they proclaim that *God raised Jesus* from the dead as an act of vindication and exultation (see Acts 2:36). But this gospel implies that Jesus can "take back his own life" (10:17-18), that is, *he can raise himself* from the dead as a demonstration that he is "equal to God" and that he has God's *eschatological power* to the full. New and bold purposes, then, are served in the narrative of Jesus' appearances in the Fourth Gospel.

Ecclesiology

Remarkable, also, is the image of the church expressed in 20:19-29. Of course, many of the traditional features are found here as well: apostolic commissionings, confirmation of the commissioning by the sending of the Holy Spirit, a

mission of repentance and forgiveness. But the Fourth
Gospel says more. As we noted in regard to the pattern of
believer preaching to an unbeliever, we gain a realistic sense
of the process which we all accept even today, namely, that
a) our faith rests on the faith of others and b) faith comes
through hearing of God's word preached in the church.
Whatever we would know of the Risen Jesus today rests on
the word of the first witnesses commissioned to preach.
And inasmuch as the commission to preach and to forgive
is circumscribed to the disciples gathered together, the gospel
gives the sense of a specific covenant community attempting
to be clear about leadership roles and the localization of
authority in it. The church which comes to faith, moreover,
is led to a full confession of Jesus, not merely as the vindicated Son of Man or as the suffering Christ, but as the one
who is "equal to God" and "Lord and God." This resurrection narrative, then, defines the church, indicating specific
roles in it, the legitimacy of its central task (forgiveness,
preaching), the process of its mission, and the fullness of its
faith.

7

John 21:1-24
"Jesus and Peter, the New Shepherd"

It is generally agreed that the original ending of the Fourth Gospel came right after the appearance to Thomas in 20:30-31. Yet we have another chapter of the gospel which records an extended appearance of Jesus in Jn 21:1-24, a narrative which was apparently added to the Fourth Gospel at a later stage of its redaction. Although we are accustomed to investigate the Easter appearances of the Risen Jesus with him as the primary focus, that would not be the best way to understand what is being communicated in 21:1-24; for the narrative there wants to discuss the relative importance of two leaders in the Johannine community, Peter and the Beloved Disciple. Church issues crowd in on strictly christological issues. Let us, then, look at what Jesus has to say vis-à-vis these two important figures in this early christian community.

Redaction

We cannot understand Chapter 21 independently of the rest of the gospel because the evangelist presumes that we are conversant with the whole of the text and know all about the cast of characters before we begin the story. As considerate readers, let us briefly summarize what the author of the Fourth Gospel expects us to know as we begin to read John 21. Basically, he wants us to recall all we know about Peter and the Beloved Disciple.

Peter. Although the synoptic gospels indicate that Peter was chosen first of Jesus' disciples and made rock of Jesus' followers (see Mk 1:16-18; Mt 4:18-20; Lk 5:1-11), that is not how the Fourth Gospel tells the story. In John's gospel, Peter is called second, after his brother Andrew and another unnamed disciple spent time with Jesus. A small point, but since it flies in the face of the tradition, it is an important, initial statement about Peter in this particular gospel. He is called, moreover, not by Jesus himself, but by Andrew. Furthermore, whereas in the synoptic gospels Peter utters the great confession that Jesus is the Christ (Mk 8:29//Lk 9:20//Mt 16:16) and is even acclaimed the charismatic leader of Jesus' followers because of that confession (Mt 16:17-19), the possible counterpart to this triumphant event in the Fourth Gospel puts Peter in a decidedly weaker light. The occasion is the apostasy of disciples, not their acclamation of Jesus as Prophet (Jn 6:60-66); Peter and the other disciples are not asked what they think of Jesus, but "Will you also go away?" (6:67); Peter's response is not the inspired confession of Jesus as "Christ," but a remark that could indicate timidity, "To whom shall we go?" (6:68). Instead of confessing Jesus as "Christ," Peter merely describes him as "the Holy one of God" (6:69), a remark not much different from what the timid Nicodemus had earlier said of Jesus (3:2).

Before his Farewell Discourse (Jn 14-17), Jesus washed the feet of his disciples, a gesture which not only suggested service (13:12-16) but symbolized ritual washing for sacrifice. Peter protested to this preparatory washing (13:6-8), which prompted Jesus to remark that Peter was surely "not in the know," that he is ignorant of important matters, a highly prejudicial slur in this gospel: "What I am doing you do not know now" (13:7). And in fact, Peter was *not* ready for sacrifice or bold following of Jesus or fearless confession of him. Jesus predicts of Peter that he will deny him three times (13:36-38 and 18:17, 25-27). Peter, moreover, lacks special and secret information, such as the identity of the traitor, for which he must depend on the Beloved Disciple, who is truly intimate with Jesus (13:24-26). Again and again, therefore, Peter is cast in unfavorable light: 1) as one "not in the know," 2) as one who is not fearless in following Jesus, and 3) as one who is not called first.

Beloved Disciple. In contrast with Peter, the Beloved Disciple is always cast as one "in the know," bold and fearless in crisis situations, and an intimate of Jesus. First, he does not appear on the scene until the Farewell Address, a time of crisis for Jesus' disciples; and in that context he is most favorably portrayed. He is "the one whom Jesus loved" (13:23-26; see 19:26; 20:2), which is symbolized by his physical and spiritual closeness to Jesus, "lying close to the breast of Jesus" (13:23). He has, moreover, the most important knowledge at the time, the identity of the traitor (13:25-26). Second, he boldly follows Jesus, not only into the very prison and courtroom of Jesus (18:15-16), but also to his cross, the only one of the disciples to be publicly associated with the condemned Jesus (19:25-27). On that climactic occasion, Jesus declares him his brother ("Woman, behold your son!") and bonds him to his own mother ("Behold your mother!"), another indication of the great status of this figure (19:25-27). Even on Easter morning, he is subtly described as Peter's superior: he runs "faster," he gets to the tomb "first," and he "saw and believed" (20:8), actions and insights which are not credited to Peter, but which cast the Beloved Disciple as a figure superior to Peter in every respect.

In fact, the Fourth Gospel has repeatedly presented the Beloved Disciple as the foil of Peter. Concerning Judas the Traitor, Peter is *not* "in the know," whereas the Beloved Disciple knows. This Beloved Disciple arranges for Peter to follow him into the high priest's quarters, where he, not Peter, remains faithful. He, not Peter, is at Jesus' cross; and he, not Peter "sees and believes" at Jesus' tomb. Shall we call them rivals? At least we should be aware of the consistent characterization of them as contrasting figures as we approach John 21, where we find them compared and contrasted once more. It is my sugggestion that John 21 consciously takes up the various contrasts between Peter and the Beloved Disciple, but this time tells the story so that on every point, Peter is uplifted and restored to the position he enjoys in the traditions of the early church. John 21, then, stands as a corrective to the gospel, as a final attempt to make it more traditional and more in line with the other apostolic churches. The Risen Jesus, therefore, restores the fortunes of Peter and makes him the only shepherd of Jesus' flock, a bold apologetic move.

Structure & Form

John 21 is a complicated narrative containing a number of scenes and motifs:

A. 21:1-14   Peter's miraculous catch of fish
B. 21:15-17   commissioning of Peter
C. 21:18-19   prophecy about Peter
D. 21:20-24   a final controversy between Peter
               and the Beloved Disciple

In general, it can be said that the unifying element of John 21 resides in the figure of Peter, who is the chief fisherman, the one whom Jesus makes shepherd of the flock, about whom Jesus predicts a martyr's death, and finally whose death seems to contrast him with the Beloved Disciple's supposed deathlessness. Yet, all of Jesus' actions in this final resurrection appearance serve to confirm Peter's role in the church.

Miraculous Catch. The new appearance of Jesus narrated at the end of this gospel the type of incident one finds in the synoptic gospels at the beginning of Jesus' career in Galilee. And in fact, Jn 21:1-14 is quite similar in many ways to the account in Lk 5:1-11 which narrates Luke's version of the initial call of Peter.

Luke 5:1-11	*John 21:1-14*
1. setting: Jesus' earthly ministry: teaching the crowds	1. setting: Jesus' post-resurrection ministry: commissioning
2. dramatis personae: Peter and Andrew, James and John	2. dramatis personae: Peter, beloved Disciple, Thomas, Nathanael, Zebedee's sons, and two others
3. miracle: -fished all night & caught nothing -at Jesus' command -a great catch -nets begin to break	3. miracle: -fished all night & caught nothing -at Jesus' command -a great catch -nets do not begin to break
4.———	4. meal with Jesus
5. Peter's confession: "I am a sinful man"	5. Peter's confession: triple protestation of loyalty balancing Peter's triple denial of Jesus
6. commission: "Henceforth you will be catching men"	6. commission: "Feed my lambs, feed my sheep"

Probably the author of this final chapter of John knew of the tradition of Peter, the fisherman, commissioned to special leadership by Jesus. He drew upon that hallowed story as the framework for this special addition to the Fourth Gospel which so clearly affirms Peter's role as both chief Fisherman as well as principal Shepherd of Jesus' flock. As it does in the synoptic tradition, the miraculous catch of fish symbolizes the mission to which Peter and the other disciples are commissioned, a mission expressed later

in pastoral terms of shepherd and flock. The point of this is
to underscore the consistent function of Jesus' resurrection
manifestations as church commissionings.

Yet reviewing Jn 21:1-14 in the light of previous incidents
in the Fourth Gospel, we can see how the author intends us
to see here a reversal of roles between Peter and the Beloved
Disciple. Now it is Peter who shows intiative ("I am going
fishing," 21:3); although the Beloved Disciple continues to
have special insight ("It is the Lord," 21:7a), Peter takes
over the role of intimate and swims to Jesus (21:7b). In
place of the farewell meal, there is a meal of fish and bread
at which Peter and Jesus serve (21:9-12). Initiative, passion,
respect and service now characterize Peter, virtues he did
not display at the farewell supper. The appearance of the
Risen Jesus, then, becomes the occasion to begin the
restoration of Peter along more traditional lines.

Commissioning. The next scene belongs exclusively to
Peter and Jesus. Its structure contains a triple question,
answer and commissioning:

1. Question:	2. Answer:	3. Commission
"Simon, son of John,	"Yes, Lord; you	"Feed my lambs"
do you love me more	know that I love	"Tend my sheep"
than these?"	you."	"Feed my sheep"
(21:15a, 16a, 17a)	21:15b, 16b, 17b)	(21:15c, 16c, 17c)

Considerate readers of the gospel recognize that the question-answer form is intended to offset the triple denial of
Jesus by Peter earlier in the Passion Narrative (13:38; 18:27).
When we stop to think about it, the New Testament often
describes a significant person or leader in the early church
by recalling his former sins. Matthew is remembered as the
former Tax Collector; Mary Magdalene, the one out of
whom Jesus drove seven demons; Paul, the persecutor of
the church; Peter, of course, will always be remembered as
the apostle who denied the Lord. Yet Matthew is an apostle;
Mary, a celebrated disciple; Paul, the apostle to the Gentile;

and Peter, the Shepherd of Jesus' flock.

Shepherd. Considerate readers are also expected to recall earlier remarks by Jesus about "shepherds" and "sheep." An **authentic** and **noble** shepherd is one who "lays down his life for the sheep" (10:11,15); he enters by the door, the ordinary entrance, for he is no interloper, no pseudo-leader (10:1-2); he calls the sheep by name and leads them out (10:3). Yet in acclaiming Peter as shepherd, Jesus also predicts in 21:18-19 that Peter the shepherd will demonstrate the chief characteristic of a noble shepherd, viz., that he will "lay down his life," a thing repulsive to the Peter of John 13, 18 and 19.

And in his commission to be the official shepherd of the Johannine flock, Peter reverses a role which has been assumed earlier by the Beloved Disciple. When the Beloved Disciple and Peter followed Jesus to the court of the high priest, a considerable amount of attention was given to the ability of the Beloved Disciple to negotiate doors: 1) he can enter through the door, and 2) he can make it possible for others to enter through that door. It is not farfetched to see here an allusion to the parable of the shepherd in 10:1-5.

Parable in 10:1-5	*Events in 18:15-16*
1. "He who enters by the door is the shepherd of the sheep" (10:2)	1. "As this disciple was known to the high priest he entered ... while Peter stood outside at the door" (18:15)
2. "To him the gate-keeper opens" (10:3)	2. "So the other disciple ... spoke to the maid who kept the door ..." (18:16)
3. "He calls his own sheep by name and leads them out" (10:3b)	3. " ... and brought Peter in" (18:16b)

On that occasion, the Beloved Disciple was cast in the role
of shepherd, with Peter as sheep. But in 21:15-17 the roles
are reversed, as Peter is officially declared shepherd of
Jesus' sheep and lambs, implying that he is even shepherd to
the Beloved Disciple. Jn 21:15-17, then, expects us to recall
(a) the triple denial by Peter as well as (b) the shepherd
imagery in 10:1-5 and 18:15-16. In the dialogue by the lake
in Galilee, Jesus (a) formally counters Peter's triple denial
with a triple confession of loyalty and (b) commissions him
to play the role of shepherd to Jesus' flock, both in leadership and in laying down his life. The Risen Jesus restores
Peter's status in the Johannine church with this solemn
commissioning. Peter is the premier fisherman and the chief
shepherd.

Prophecy. In 21:18-19 we find a remarkable phenomenon,
a prophecy made by the Risen Jesus. Luke indicated in 24:6
and 44 that all the important teaching and discourse on
Easter Sunday was but a clearer understanding of what the
earthly Jesus had said over and over during his ministry,
but which had not been understood by the dense disciples.
In Jn 21:18-19, however, we have a fresh statement by
Jesus, even a prophecy of future events. Jesus predicts a
martyr's death for Peter, the shepherd. This prophecy, of
course, asks us to recall how in the gospel itself there were
heroes and cowards. Heroes, like the man born blind,
confess Jesus even at the cost of being expelled from the
synagogue (9:34), whereas cowards, like this man's parents
(9:22-23) and many of the authorities (12:42), were afraid to
acknowledge Jesus for fear of reprisals which might include
death as well as excommunication (see 16:1-3). In this light,
Peter does not fare well, for when the symbolic washing was
offered him by Jesus, a washing which prepares for sacrifice
and death, Peter completely refused ("You shall never wash
my feet," 13:8). And when the time came for him publicly to
acknowledge his loyalty to Jesus, three times he denied the
Lord. By the logic of the gospel, Peter would be linked with
cowards, and so lose face and standing in the group. All the
more remarkable, then, is the prophecy of Jesus that Peter,

after all, will be loyal unto death, even the death of a confessing witness, i.e. a martyr. And in this death, he will exemplify one more characteristic of the role of shepherd in which Jesus has just cast him. Like a noble shepherd, he will lay down his life for Jesus' sheep. In this light, then, Peter no longer plays the role of coward to the Beloved Disciple's hero. He becomes a Johannine hero in his own right.

Controversy. The dialogue between Peter and the Risen Lord in John 21 concludes with the resolution of one last point of rivalry between Peter and the Beloved Disciple. Jn 21:20-24 stand in sharp contrast to 21:18-19. In the former verses, Jesus predicts Peter's death, which is perceived as a good thing ("Jesus said this to show by what death he was to glorify God," 21:19), but in the latter verses, it is assumed that one is better if one does *not die* (21:23). And so in some way the Beloved Disciple would still be "better" than Peter because, unlike Peter, he would appear as a figure who will never die. A final conflict in the gospel, then, arises as Peter is once more contrasted with the Beloved Disciple, now in terms of dying versus not dying.

If the figure of Peter has been formally elevated by Jesus in 21:1-19, the question is finally and explicitly raised about the status of the Beloved Disciple: "Lord, what about this man?" (21:21). The shape of this part of the narrative is characterized by a pattern which is part and parcel of the discourses of Jesus throughout the Fourth Gospel: Jesus makes an initial **statement,** which is **misunderstood** by his listeners, and which prompts a final **clarification** by Jesus.

Statement	Misunderstanding	Explanation
3:3	3:4	3:5
4:10	4:11	4:12
11:11	11:12	11:13-15
14:4	14:5	14:6
16:25-26	16:29-30	16:31-33

In light of this pattern, Jesus' **statement** about the Beloved Disciple was: "If it is my will that he remain until I come, what is that to you?" (21:22), which was **misunderstood** by some in the Johannine community as "This disciple was not to die" (21:23a). This **misunderstanding**, moreover, takes the typical form of other misunderstandings in the Fourth Gospel both by misquoting Jesus and by interpreting his words too literally. Hostile listeners misquote Jesus' works in 8:52, and so understand them too literally.

8:51	*8:52*
"If anyone keeps my words, he will never **see death**"	"If anyone keeps my words, he will never **taste death**"

Other listeners take Jesus' words too literally, such as the Samaritan woman to whom Jesus offered "living water" (4:10-15) or the disciples who hear of Lazarus' "sleep" (11:11-15). The clarification offered in 21:23 simply corrects the misunderstanding with an exact repetition of Jesus' remarks about the Beloved Disciple, "Yet Jesus did *not* say that he was not to die, but 'If it is my will that he remain until I come, what is that to you?'"

It is not clear whether the Christians who passed on this narrative knew whether the Beloved Disciple had died or was still alive. But, either way, his possible "deathlessness" should not be construed as a criterion for elevating him above Peter. The very raising, however, of the issue in this particular narrative where Peter is so evidently restored to primacy indicates both that it was a controversial point, even a point still used to prefer the Beloved Disciple over Peter, and a point presumably settled by the Risen Lord himself. At least certain **misunderstandings** of Jesus' words are exposed and criticized. Internal tensions in the Johannine group seem to have lasted and lasted, without any clear resolution.

Christology

Although the focus of this narrative was not as evidently on Jesus as it was in stories such as Mt 28:16-20 and Lk 24:36-49, there are many important aspects of the identity and role of the Risen Jesus expressed in Jn 21:1-24. Jesus, of course, formally commissions a disciple to special ministry to his flock, a traditional function of resurrection appearances. Yet Jn 21:1-24 is different in that only Peter is so commissioned here, not the Twelve (see Jn 20:19-23). In some respects, this might be John's version of an ancient tradition that Jesus "appeared to Simon" apart from the other disciples (see Lk 23:34; 1 Cor 15:5). Jesus, and Jesus alone, exercises lasting authority over the covenant community as the appointer of authentic leaders of the church. The forthright but delicate way that Jesus elicits a triple protestation of loyalty from Peter illustrates the traditional notion of Jesus as the one who forgives sins (see the commission to forgive sins in 20:22-23). By eating a meal with Peter and others (21:9-13), Jesus demonstrates once more that it is his continued pleasure to "eat with tax collectors and sinners." Finally, Jesus remains the definitive teacher of his flock, for he prophesies of Peter's death. Further Jesus clarifies misunderstandings of his earlier words. One might say that Jn 21:1-24, while distinctively Johannine in the way it tells the story, is also very traditional in the role Jesus plays in this account, especially in his commission of Peter as chief shepherd of the flock.

Ecclesiology

As we noted earlier, the figure of Peter not only holds together all of the pieces of Jn 21:1-24, but constitutes the editorial focus. As we noted with the figure of Thomas, the *dramatis personae* of the Fourth Gospel are presented in the narrative as representative types or embodiments of characteristic actions or insights. Thomas, who was so befuddled by Jesus' earlier discourses on death and survival of death, typifies the ideal disciple who makes the superb confession of Jesus' divinity because of his ability to transcend death, "My Lord and my God." The man born blind, because of his fearless confession of Jesus in the face of threats of excommunication from the synagogue (9:22), becomes the archetypal witness to Jesus (cf. 12:42). So, too, Peter and the Beloved Disciple represent types of leaders corresponding to types of communities which appear to have been in conflict, even in the Johannine church.

1. Peter, of course, represents traditional, apostolic leadership (*ascribed* leadership), whereas the Beloved Disciple typifies charismatic or *achieved* leadership.

2. Peter received a special leadership name, "Rock" (Jn 1:42; Mt 16:18); his church commissioning by Jesus transformed his profession as a fisherman into a symbol of his office, for he became a "Fisher of Men" (Mk 1:17; Lk 5:10; Jn 21:1-14). The very name "Beloved Disciple" only tells us that he was an intimate of Jesus; if he can be said to have any leadership role, it is that of a personal "intimate" of Jesus, first with Jesus and then with Jesus' mother, although he is never said to have this relationship with other Johannine Christians. His status is extemely high nonetheless.

3. Peter's role is based first on a word from the earthly Jesus (1:42) and finally on a revelation from the Risen Lord (21:15-17); his *ascribed* leadership, moreover, somehow rests on his being an eyewitness of all that Jesus did and said. On the other hand, the Beloved Disciple's position is *achieved* by virtue of his intimacy with Jesus, his ability to be in the know (13:25-26), his fearless, public following of Jesus, especially in crisis situations (18:15-16; 19:25-26), and finally his independence of material proofs and arguments (20:8). The very possibility that the Beloved Disciple may never die is one more instance of this charismatic qualification.

4. Peter's function, at least in the general New Testament tradition, is that of preacher of the deeds and sayings of the earthly Jesus; he is a foundation stone for the group

gathered in memory and honor of Jesus. The Beloved Disciple, however, is important for the special information and secrets he is privy to, not the tradition of the public deeds and sayings of the earthly Jesus. If Peter represents the "past," the Beloved Disciple stands for the "future" and for what is novel.

If we are correct in interpreting Peter and the Beloved Disciple as types of leaders, we should push the inquiry one step further and ask about the types of communities they represent. Peter obviously would represent more traditional New Testament communities with clearly identified roles and leaders, whose task is to hand on the tradition about Jesus and to be faithful to the past. Peter represents a community in which the sense of group identity was stronger than the individualism of significant members within the group. One might call such persons "conservative," if by that one meant a leader who was faithful to the earthly Jesus and the traditions of the early church. The Beloved Disciple, however, seems to represent a strong sense of individualism which, because of the many deliberate contrasts with Peter, is seen in competition with traditional leadership. Not privy to the deeds and discourses of the earthly Jesus, he is not their servant; not known for his sharing of Jesus' ministry, he is not bound to it, but looks to what is new and future. What he claims to know from Jesus may be quite esoteric, and there is no testing the truth of his knowledge the way "Peter's" preaching could be matched against the reports of other eyewitnesses (see 1 Jn 1:1-4).

The Fourth Gospel evidently reflects a christian community containing two types of groups with two types of leaders, a conflict reflected quite clearly in the Johannine epistles. But in John 21, while the community restores Peter, it does not do so by denigrating the Beloved Disciple. On the contrary, the very things that made the Beloved Disciple such an attractive leader are credited to Peter as well: a) special intimacy with Jesus (21:7), b) special knowledge from Jesus (21:18-19), and c) special "shepherd" role (21:15-17). Peter's *ascribed* role is buttressed by his *achieve-*

ments vis-à-vis the Risen Jesus. Peter not only becomes the premier shepherd, but he becomes a unity figure who blends into one person different styles of being a follower of Jesus and different values. In one person, concern for "past" and "future" are wedded; in one person, the words and deeds of the earthly Jesus are joined with the revelations of the Risen Christ.

The very presence of John 21 in the gospel indicates that the Johannnine community was a complex group with serious internal tensions. John 21, moreover, attempts to redress the perceived competition and rivalry between Peter and the Beloved Disciple in favor of Peter and traditional leadership roles in which there can be unity and harmony. But in so doing, the author of John 21 performed a diplomatic job of not banishing the Beloved Disciple and the type of status which he represents. After all, the Beloved Disciple is the first to recognize Jesus ("It is the Lord," 21:7) and he still enjoys the reputation of Jesus' remark that he might "remain until I come" (21:23). The Risen Jesus, of course, moderates the conflict, corrects the misunderstandings, and settles the issue of the internal unity and structure of the church by his restoration of Peter. After all, "the net was not torn" (21:11). If the Risen Lord might be said to launch the church by his commissionings in Mt 28:16-20 and Lk 24:44-47, in the Fourth Gospel he steadies the church on its course, giving mid-course corrections. The Risen Jesus, then, remains present to the church as its eternal Lord.

Conclusion

The survey of the stories of Jesus' resurrection in this brief study leads us to reflect on some of the common themes or emphases in them.

Form and Function. Knowledge of the vocation-call narrative form, which stands behind Mt 28:16-20; Lk 24:44-49; Jn 20:19-23, proved to be truly useful. For the reader of these stories can appreciate how the resurrection appearances of Jesus were preached and perceived as events at which Jesus commissioned certain persons to a leadership role in the church. The stories function, then, to structure the new covenant community of disciples, establishing roles and offices, legitimating authority in the group and conferring status on important individuals for service to the group.

Variation. Although all of the stories attempt to tell to the whole church the common importance of Jesus' appearance to particular individuals, the narratives studied here cannot but be examined vis-à-vis the specific audience and church addressed. Paul crafted his remarks in 1 Cor 15:3-8 as apologetic correction to pneumatic excesses in Corinth, just as the author of John 21 is concerned in his church with internal tensions between two types of leaders and two kinds of church structures. The more attention we give to the specific church addressed and its particular issues, the richer becomes our sense of the pastoral concerns that went into each version of the resurrection stories.

Growth and Development. Comparing the bare list in 1 Cor 15:5-8 with the detailed narrative in Lk 24 and John 20-21, we begin to appreciate how the basic message of early Christian preachers was later cast into narrative form with dramatic exchanges and vivid details. We begin to appreciate the observation that this development does not depend so much on the evangelists' recovery of historial details as on their casting of the story in terms typical of the way they tell the whole gospel narrative. Each evangelist attempted in his version of the Easter appearances of Jesus to indicate the continuity of that story with the rest of the gospel, how the Jesus of history relates to the Christ of faith. Most of the narrative details, then, might be seen as coming from each evangelist's own particular way of preaching the gospel.

Christology. In this survey, we have come to see how each narrative of Jesus' resurrection appearances also serves as a compendium of the major statements about Jesus which the evangelist or author attempts to make throughout the gospel itself. The stories, then, function as summaries of each evangelist's christology: Jesus is the universal Lord (Mt), Shepherd of his flock (Lk 24:13-36; Jn 21), the saving Jesus who continues to eat with sinners and call them to repentance, as he did in his earthly ministry (Lk 24:36-49). He is the premier giver of the Holy Spirit (Jn 20:22), the forgiver of sins (Lk 24:47; Jn 20:23). And he is most assuredly "Lord and God" (Jn 20:28).

Ecclesiology. Most importantly, this survey has shown that the narratives cannot speak about Jesus without at the same time speaking about the group of Jesus' disciples, which is the church. Christ is community. And the resurrection stories tell of his commissioning of specific persons to specific roles, tasks and offices in the covenant community gathered in his name. They tell, moreover, of the nature of the church, the scope of its membership, the extent of its mission, the substance of its confession and the process of its faith. Furthermore, we learn about specific churches, their problems and tensions and how the early church invoked the risen and present Lord to resolve them. The preaching about Jesus in the resurrection stories, then, should be seen as part of the direct pastoral care of the early churches, for the message is always shaped and crafted to address real issues in those churches.

Further Reading

Brown, Raymond E., *The Virginal Conception and Bodily Resurrection of Jesus* (New York: Paulist, 1973)

Cadbury, Henry J., "Rebuttal, A Submerged Motive in the Gospels," *Quantulacumque Studies in Honor of Kirsopp Lake* (ed. R.P. Casey and Silva Lake; London: Christophers, 1937) 99-108

Dillon, Richard, *From Eye-Witnesses to Ministers of the Word. Tradition and Composition in Luke 24* (AnB 80; Rome: Biblical Institute Press, 1978)

——————, "Easter Revelation and Mission Program in Luke 24:46-48," *Sin, Salvation and the Spirit* 240-270

Dodd, C.H., "The Appearances of the Risen Christ: An Essay in Form-Criticism of the Gospels," *Studies in the Gospels* (Oxford: Blackwell, 1957) 9-35

Fitzmyer, Joseph, The Gospel According to Luke (AB 28A; Garden City: Doubleday, 1985) 1532-1586

Fuller, Reginald, *The Formation of the Resurrection Narratives* (New York: Macmillan, 1971)

Hubbard, Benjamin, *The Matthean Redaction of a Primitive Apostolic Commissioning: An Exegesis of Matthew 28:16-20* (SBLDS 19: Missoula MT: Scholars Press, 1974)

Kingsbury, Jack D., "The Composition and Christology of Mt 28:16-20," *Journal of Biblical Literature* 93 (1974) 573-584

Kloppenborg, John, "An Analysis of the Pre-Pauline Formula 1 Cor 15:3b-5 in Light of Some Recent Literature," *Catholic Biblical Quarterly* 40 (1978) 351-367

Legrand, L., "Christ the Fellow Traveller. The Emmaus Story in Lk 24:13-35," *Indian Theological Studies* 19 (1982) 33-44

Minear, Paul, "We Do Not Know Where ... Jn 20:2," *Interpretation* 30 (1976) 125-139

O'Collins, Gerald, *What Are They Saying About the Resurrection?* (New York: Paulist, 1978)

Perkins, Pheme, *Resurrection. New Testament Witness and Contemporary Reflection* (Garden City: Doubleday, 1984)

Schubert, Paul, "The Structure and Significance of Luke 24," *Neutestamentliche Studien für Rudolf Bultmann* (Göttingen: Vandenhoeck and Ruprecht, 1954) 165-184

Schnackenburg, Rudolf, *The Gospel According to St. John* (New York: Crossroads, 1982) 300-374

Scripture Index

Scripture Index

OLD TESTAMENT

NEW TESTAMENT